LET YOUR SOUL
EVOLVE

Spiritual Growth for the New Millennium

SECOND EDITION

PHIL DIAZ & P.D. ALLEVA

with:
Antonio T. de Nicolas,
Maria Maddalena Colavito,
M.M. Barrett

let your soul evolve
be awakened

The authors of this book do not dispense medical advice or pre-scribe the use of any technique as a form of treatment for physical, emotional, or medical problems without the advice of a physician, either directly or indirectly. The intent of the authors is only to offer information of a general nature to help you in your quest for emo-tional and spiritual well-being. In the event you use any of the infor-mation in this book for yourself, which is your constitutional right, the authors and publisher assume no responsibility for your actions.

Let Your Soul Evolve:
Spiritual Growth for the New Millennium
Second Edition

Copyright ©2014 Let Your Soul Evolve LLC

ISBN 978-1622-873-03-6 PRINT

LCCN 2014946936

July 2014

Published and Distributed by
First Edition Design Publishing, Inc.
P.O. Box 20217, Sarasota, FL 34276-3217
www.firsteditiondesignpublishing.com

Spiritual Practice as Healing by Antonio de Nicolas used with permis-sion of the author.

Ancient Greek Philosopher-Physicians and Early Foundations of Spiritual Growth Therapy by Maria Maddalena Colavito used with permission of the author.

Editing: Candace Johnson
Cover art: Shawn Dall
Cover design: Tyler Kuethe
Interior design: Gary A. Rosenberg

CONTENTS

*For my wife, Lisa,
without whom this book
would never have been written.
Thank you for opening
the universe to me.*

—P.D. ALLEVA

*To my beloved partner
in life, Molena Mia,
the woman who inspires me
to be the best I can be
and reminds me always
to put God first.*

—PHIL DIAZ

*There is no place in our brains, our lives or the
universe for any negative recordings so let them go . . .
observe, obtain, absorb, and record
beautiful peace and love.*

—SPENCER KINARD

Acknowledgments

The authors would like to acknowledge the following people for helping to write and complete this book, without whom this project would never have been completed:

Marnie Barrett, whose passion and patience and drive made it possible to tie up all the loose ends needed for publication;

Antonio de Nicolas and Maria Maddalena Colavito for graciously sharing their wisdom;

Will Allen, P. J. Greene, and Katie Forlano for their insight and help;

All clients and employees of Lifescape Solutions, whose belief in the authors has been inspirational;

Candace Johnson, our editor, for curbing our passions and inconsistencies to help put out a viable and professional product;

Our families for putting up with our deadlines and supporting our passions for getting our message out to the world.

PREFACE

The mind is everything.
What you think you become.
—BUDDHA

THIS BOOK IS ABOUT HEALING that does not just solve symptoms, but leads to the evolution of your soul. While there is nothing new in the specific information contained in it, this book presents a new view of our role in the world. In this view, we are the authors of our lives. There are many people in this twenty-first century who know about and even agree with the point of view presented in this book. What has been lacking is the application of this knowledge to the healing practices that are entrenched in an old paradigm, one in which we are simply helpless organisms with little control over our own well-being. As a society, we have been cowed by a mechanistic view of the world in which we are little more than animated machines with little power over our lives.

We, the authors, do not hold to that view, and today we offer a new view that incorporates all our historical knowledge, validates the importance of our own intuition, and accepts the power of belief and the ability to heal ourselves. With it, we offer you a chance to become free and to become the author of your own fate.

This new view is called Spiritual Growth Therapy, and it is a method of psychological healing that uses the science of vibrational healing, manifestation, philosophy, native healing from all cultures, Ayurvedic medicine, hypnosis, and current psychology. With Spiritual Growth Therapy, we challenge the idea that there is just one right way to work with people who have psychological issues.

It is your choice to find which practices work for you. It is up to you to define how you want to improve your life. In our view, all any healer can do is offer as many options as possible for you to choose from.

For centuries, religion has offered people the chance for new lives, forgiveness, and support. Beginning in the last century, the power of religion, faith, and God was discounted by the pseudointellectuals who have come to dominate our cultural point of view. This has continued, even in the face of factual evidence that the majority of people on the planet believe in the power of faith.

In the medical field, the powers of prayer and positive thinking have finally been acknowledged. We have all heard of medical miracles that occurred when a sick person sought treatment from a traditional healer, energy worker, or herbalist. We often discount these stories when we hear them and do not incorporate these possibilities into our thinking about healing.

This is even truer in the psychological fields. The medical model has a stranglehold on the practice of psychology. But that wasn't always true. In the 1960s and '70s, the movement toward existential psychotherapy moved the psychological field toward a different paradigm. One of those who chose to challenge the assumption that mental illness, especially schizophrenia, was more an expression of social distress than a medical problem was psychiatrist R.D. Laing, who postulated that for many schizophrenics, the experience is transformative, understandable, and useful (Laing 1960).

In my own practice as a therapist (with supposedly mentally ill people), I have learned that many patients can cope with their supposed symptoms but have problems with the way the world around them responds to those symptoms.

In short, it's not the hallucinations that are the "problem," but the way society views those hallucinations. Laing was revolutionary in valuing the content of psychotic or schizophrenic behavior as a valid response to an untenable situation; "Insanity," he said, "is a perfectly rational adjustment to an insane world" (Laing 1960). He saw psychosis as a spiritual experience, one we could all learn from if we could learn the language and symbolism of the psychotic.

This has also been said of drug-induced experiences, which have been used in traditional societies for centuries as a method toward enlightenment. Of course, in those societies we are not talking about recreational drug use, but about guided experiences led by experienced healers.

Rollo May, MD, said, "Every human being must have some point at which he stands against the culture, where he says, this is me and the damned world can go to hell" (May 1953). In a conformist society, the individual is often punished for making choices that don't fit into mainstream thinking. In fact, the healthy people are often the ones who rebel against such a toxic society that demands conformity.

In both May and Laing we see that our definitions of mental health are judged by the social norms of behavior. We are, after all, seen and judged in our social context. Many existential therapists support the notion that therapy can be oppressive if the goal is to make the patient socially compliant. Therefore, it is important to ensure that we do not violate the personal journey the patient takes on his or her way to self-knowledge.

In this context, we must be careful to use medication sparingly and not just to control patients' behaviors. It is, after all, up to the individual to choose his path in life, even if that decision includes suicide or madness. It is our contention that psychotherapy should have the goals of symptom reduction and self-actualization. It is all up to the individual to choose the quality of his or her life.

One great example of the power of individual decision-making on mental health and spiritual growth—even in the face of death—is Dr. Victor Frankl, a concentration camp survivor. In his book *Man's Search for Meaning*, Frankl describes life in a concentration camp from the viewpoint of a psychiatrist. Frankl postulates that all suffering has meaning, and love is the ultimate redemption (Frankl 1946, 2006).

Two decades later, Frankl wrote *The Doctor and the Soul*, which opened new bridges between psychiatry and philosophy and reminded us that our search for ourselves, our place in the world, and the love we give others are all part of the human experience. While that search is sometimes anxiety producing and leaves us distressed, it is also unavoidable as part of the human experience (Frankl 1967).

Because of the slow acceptance of new paradigms by existing institutions, much of what we discuss in this book is still not offered to the general public in any meaningful way. It is our intention to change that and make it possible for everyone to have a legitimate alternative to generally accepted psychological practice.

Spiritual Growth Therapy (SGT) is a new paradigm rooted in ancient knowledge. This book is not in any way a definitive discussion of SGT options, but the beginning of a discussion about alternative healing options. It is our purpose to make this an open discussion to be continued on our website http://letyoursoulevolve.com. Updated versions and additional volumes of this book will be published, and the whole planet will be invited to contribute.

We invite shamans, priests, poets, traditional medicine practitioners, vibrational healers, chiropractors, trance mediums, angel workers, and anyone who practices a healing art to visit our website and start a planetary discussion.

Much has been written about the potentially oppressive nature of current mental health practice. So much of current therapeutic practice is coercive, and its goal is to make the patient more socially acceptable. We believe there is a better way.

We are engaged in a great experiment to create a fully open system of growth options in a mental health setting that offers personal options for healing. We are committed to opening up the therapeutic process to all that is available in the helping arena. To this end, the coauthors of this book offer treatment programs that utilize Spiritual Growth

Therapy. They are Lifescape Solutions Treatment Center (http://lifescapesolutions.com) and Let Your Self Evolve Mental Health clinics (http://www.letyoursoulevolve.com/counseling-therapy-services/). We are not looking for submission to social norms; we are aiming to help our clients reach enlightenment. We invite you to join us in creating a new movement for healing!

—*Phil Diaz*

Whatever it is that we choose to occupy most of our thoughts is what we eventually identify with and what we become. This is the essence of the fifth dimension, the solidification into physical properties of all our thoughts, both alpha and omega, yin and yang, good and bad.

—P.D. ALLEVA

PART ONE

A History
of Healing

1

HEART CONSCIOUSNESS

All you need is love.
—JOHN LENNON

Over time, we humans have learned to use our brains to make decisions as we attempt to view the world through the eyes of logic. We've searched for a rational, cognitive understanding of the way we think that affects the outcome of an action. However, this practice has turned into a solidification of the brain, as if someone poured wet concrete into our skulls, and the result has turned us into hardheaded, unemotional robots for whom logic and rationale have been misconstrued to fit the needs and ego of the person who is doing the thinking and the acting.

At the very foundation of Spiritual Growth Therapy is heart consciousness: viewing the world through the actions of the heart, and in essence, through the eyes of love and understanding. There can be no wrong in making decisions that are rooted in love. But we must show love by our actions;

we must exhibit love in our hearts and in our energy. Show others how to love themselves and the world, and we have completed our jobs with the heart of the almighty. This is the utopia that has been prophesized; this is how we must teach our children, to whom the task of changing the world has been given. But first, we must begin to tackle this task for ourselves.

To do so, let's begin by taking an in-depth view of the points of the triad.

THE TRIAD

BALANCE + FULFILLMENT + PURPOSE =
The embodiment of Love through the actions of the Heart.

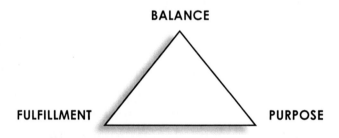

There's an additional component on a three-dimensional scale that we will get to later in this chapter, but for now we will touch on the individual points noted above.

When we first choose to heal, to understand what lies within our hearts and our emotions, to delve deep into our minds and our histories about the depths of our being, the journey in the evolution of our souls begins to accumulate within our minds and our hearts. We may ask ourselves at this point, *"What have I done?" "What can I do differently?"* or even, *"Why am I worthy of a better life?"* Although these questions are relevant, they are the wrong questions to begin with. The first and most prevalent question should be, *"Who do I want to become?"*

The question is rather simple: we all know where we've come from, but we must begin to think about and understand who we want to be, what we wish to project, how we wish to be viewed by others, what mark we want to leave on this world before drifting off into celestial silence. Within the answers to these questions—or at the very least, the contemplation of these questions—our search for meaning and for truth begins to rapidly grow and devour us like a pack of wild wolves on a piece of meat. We mistakenly focus on the wolves instead of the more significant message.

The past is like a bag of bricks we carry along like a cross to bear, as if we are all such martyrs and it is our lot to be punished. Not true! When we are finished with carrying our bag of bricks, all we have to do is set it down and be done with it. The secret is to keep only our understanding of the lessons learned from carrying the bricks while understanding first and foremost that we chose to put the bag down. This is the reward for choosing rebirth: all the lessons of our past life are at our fingertips for us to access to make good decisions in the present. Everything else is merely our subconscious wanting to understand why we chose to do things differently.

Thoughts are like little children: all they need are attention, understanding, and guidance. So provide them with such; give them an audience under a focused state of meditation, a long walk during the sunrise or sunset, quiet time in your home or room, or while sitting silently for five minutes at a time, and they will begin to subside. The way our minds work is simple: conscious thoughts are registered in the subconscious as information from which we derive our actions. Our conscious mind is the parent, and the subconscious is the child who is being taught. But we must know that it takes our subconscious time to register the new information; this is where patience and willpower come in handy. In essence, we are retraining our subconscious how to act, and until new information has solidified in our brain, the subconscious relies on the past for information about how to cope with current situations. If we choose to satisfy these past cravings, nothing will ever change because all we are doing is concretely solidifying those actions as a part of our identity.

The identity part is the most difficult to break. I'm sure you've heard the saying, "You can't teach an old dog new tricks," which is true to the extent you choose to make it true. But nothing can be farther from the truth if you train your mind to learn new tricks.

BALANCE

To what extent do we actually find balance? What are the components involved in the task? Does a black heart filled with hate and evil seek balance by exhibiting neverending love to others? Does a pure heart seek hate to find balance? How does the yin and yang affect our walk through life? Do the universe, the solar system, and the earth seek their own balance? And what are we actually seeking balance for?

I've seen those whose personas suggest well-balanced people, but even they exhibited behaviors that would call this balance into question. Should we deny our raw instincts and desires (albeit when these traits are called into question) to properly prepare ourselves for a balanced life, one filled with joy and innocence? What happens with this energy should we suppress these desires? If we merely look at our children with adoration, sheltering them from the evils of the world, what happens once they reach this world on their own? Have we done them an injustice by not allowing them to know and understand that such evils exist and helping them to be aware of them? Is this even possible?

When the grand utopia is visited upon the earth, will these evils cease to exist? There must be a better choice than the same backstabbing, petty, and hostile world we've been living in. Do we keep these evils, the devolved heart of generations past, in the world as a means to understand what true love and beauty really are? These are all questions that should never be answered by an intelligent mind but answered only through the heart.

Heart consciousness is not settling for less or compromising; it is not naivety or acting foolishly, and it is surely not acting like a sap to be taken advantage of, especially in such times as we are living now, where the fool is taken for a ride by those who present themselves as powerful, savvy, and professional. We must always remember that we are never truly manipulated by anyone; people only manipulate themselves.

Heart consciousness is determination, confidence, purpose, fulfillment, and balance. It is the balance of seeing through the daunting episodes and circumstances to retrieve a positive outcome for all who are involved, despite the self-loathing or ego-driven mind that stands as a wall to purpose. Imagine a world where people don't judge and where opportunity abounds around every corner. Imagine a world where you pass people on the street or while driving in your car, and those people are not only grateful to be in your presence but also pacified with a peaceful energy. These things are the essence of a life spent in heart consciousness.

Heart consciousness is the understanding and sixth sense of knowing when a situation, circumstance, or person's intentions are evil. It is a feeling that we must not allow such things to affect us negatively. Heart consciousness is the word of God nipping at our ear and encouraging us to turn our reactions toward a different outcome because we are one and the same with the grand architect. This architect speaks to us by way of energy to the point where we would be fools not to follow. Heart consciousness is the ability to be completely and fully self-aware with an understanding that we have not even been capable of knowing the true depths of our person and our hearts because the heart is a direct link to God. Heart consciousness pertains directly to will and willpower, to having the ability to overcome any and all adversity with a simple feeling, understanding, and sensation of love for yourself and others. This is the place where we find true balance, with the knowledge of what must be done to help ourselves heal all wounds and the practice and actions that bring us there.

FULFILLMENT

How many people do you know who lead a life that is fulfilling? We hear of teachers or social workers who complain about how little monetary compensation they receive for helping others, while simultaneously we are told how fulfilling their employment is. But does the millionaire not have access to leading a life that is fulfilling? Fulfillment is the ability to achieve your potential, desire, or promise. To lead a life that is fulfilling requires discipline, patience, and heart. Fulfillment is achieved by action related to purpose. It is the burning desire and need to do something without gain, either monetary or ego-driven, and without the infraction of wanting to be recognized for these actions. At the same time, it is something that we absolutely must do; a command seed planted in our mind's eye that we are here to service a karmic lesson through desire. It is the action related to fulfillment that leads to enrichment of the soul.

When life throws us a task or a situation we must tackle to move forward in life, and we fulfill that task and obligation, our heart receives a sense of accomplishment: this accomplishment is fulfillment.

PURPOSE

We've dedicated an entire chapter to explain purpose, so we direct you to that chapter here with just a small note on the subject. What is purpose, exactly? How do we know what our individual purpose is? What are we here to do, to accomplish, to leave behind? What is our legacy? Purpose is that burning desire to embody, pursue, and internalize what we are passionate about. It is the lifelong journey of continued, consistent, and persistent need for enrichment. It is knowing who we are with an understanding and acceptance of information downloaded to us by the grand creator. It is the soul's karmic knowledge to make right what was once wrong. Without purpose, life would have no meaning; when life seems meaningless, that purpose is just around the corner and is ready to come to fruition. Live a life of purpose—positively and remarkably. Delve deep into your heart and soul, and thrive with passion.

MIND

The additional component of the triangle is the three-dimensional aspect of the pyramid that makes life pop: our thoughts, of which we must beware, for thoughts often betray should they not be tamed with an afterthought centered on peace. Life has its ups and downs; that is the roller coaster that is human existence. However, separate from this roller coaster (which is itself its own entity), are the thoughts that drive and affect that coaster's movement. We can choose to continue to spiral downward, or we can choose the thrill of moving upward where flight sets us far above any ups and downs.

We can separate our choices of thought to either overcome them with no limits to rising so high that our hearts embody all that is life, or to continue the tumult, continue to allow the coaster to cut through our hearts so we bleed out all love. And which of these choices would you make with the understanding that it is simply a choice?

Mind (thoughts, or what we choose to think)

Simply speaking, if we consistently think that something bad will come, what should we expect to happen? But if our thoughts are positive, bright, happy, peaceful, and calm, what will we have, what will we embody, specifically in the face of adversity?

BODY AND HEART

Our three-dimensional triangle contains many parts, more than what is readily apparent to the eye, for we must always look deeper if we are to enrich our hearts and our souls. When we look at our triangle, balance, fulfillment, purpose, and mind are readily apparent, but should we include the bottom half of our triangle, we see a mirror image of the top. Constantly reflecting both yin and yang, alpha and omega, looking upon ourselves at what we've done, what we've embodied and projected. There is always a strive for balance (whether we think of it or not), always a need for fulfillment, always a purpose somewhere driven inside the chemical structure of ourselves and the universe, and of course, there is always thought. When we reflect on these points, we see ourselves. We see that which formulates and constructs our physical bodies, with our hearts in the center of these two triangles—holding us together, filtering all the negative, and incorporating all the good (again, should we choose to do so, for any drift toward the opposite can turn the heart black.) When we reflect back, we begin to develop a belief system that is tied to our identity, but what we must understand is that our identity is what we make of ourselves, what we choose to be. We can always change ourselves and our belief systems because they are choices, and choice is based on free will.

EXAMPLES

The following is a list of examples or actions that can be taken to achieve each point of heart consciousness. Our job as a practitioner, therapist, doctor, healer, spiritual guide, mystic, or facilitator is to guide our clients to achieving heart consciousness by living these ethical principles of the heart by example. The continuing chapters in this book will outline the finer points of Spiritual Growth Therapy, the heart of which is heart consciousness.

BALANCE

- Self-care

- Meditation

- Self-reflection

- Healthy nutrition

- Exercise

- Sleep

- Medication compliance (for those who truly need to be on medication)

- Journaling

- Understanding of core needs (read Abraham Maslow for a description of core needs)

- Taking responsibility for our actions

FULFILLMENT

- Helping others
- Rising to challenges
- Acceptance
- Forgiveness (of the self)
- Actions not related to ego-driven outcomes
- Setting and satisfying goals
- Exhibiting strong moral and ethical values and character

PURPOSE

- Passion
- Positive roles
- Seeking a positive identity
- Motivation
- Willpower
- Perseverance
- Actions related to your instincts surrounding what you are meant to do in life
- Never giving up: failure is not an option

MIND (THOUGHTS)

- Write down all disempowering beliefs about the self and society

- Choose to change your perception

- Say ten positive things a day about yourself and others

- Follow the decompression exercise (found in Chapter XX: Leading a Spiritual Existence)

- Understand that only you can choose to change your thoughts and how you see yourself

—*P.D. Alleva*

2

BRIDGING THE GAP BETWEEN PHILOSOPHY, PSYCHIATRY, AND PSYCHOTHERAPY

*I know I was born and I know that I'll die,
the in between is mine.*

—EDDIE VEDDER

Everyone has his or her own personal philosophy for viewing the world, reacting to adversity, and coping with everyday life. The ancients viewed philosophy in the same way as we view psychiatry and psychotherapy. In other words, they all have the same goal, molding together in a unified system with one single purpose: to purify the soul's desire for evolution.

Of course there are major differences, though, and these differences are paramount when seeking true enlightenment, freedom, peace of mind, or evolution. The distinction is the external sources. A person may wish to seek spiritual fulfillment, to become awakened to the nature of the universe and of the self; however, in what realm must this be accomplished? Let us have a quick philosophical discussion on society.

We are a society based on the external; materialism has

injected its satanic cause into the veins of the popular and in doing so has developed a common thread in the way humans look at themselves or rather, do *not* look at themselves. There's nothing wrong with keeping up with the Joneses, so to speak, but our wants and desires to own that new iPod, sports car, big-screen or 3-D television have attached themselves to our DNA—and they are not letting go. Every ounce of our being, every cell, every thought reflects on what we don't have, all the while distracting us from a pure and simple truth: *All that we have comes from within!*

LOOKING WITHIN

The meaning of that statement should be taken in two ways: first, every time we tell ourselves, "I need" or "I want," we are informing our subconscious minds that we lack something, and we're teaching our brains that we require an external source to provide us with identity; and second, we can be and have everything on the planet just by giving it a simple thought.

Although the first interpretation will be expanded on below, the second interpretation may leave some readers slightly puzzled, as it may seem contradictory to the point. To provide some clarification: the meaning is rather simple. Nothing in this life is off-limits, and everything is yours while nothing is yours; if you think it, it will come. The point is to not allow external sources to define who you are, and this is a thought process that takes us back to the first interpretation.

We've become a society hinged on desire: everywhere we look and everything we experience is filtered through the Internet, television, movies, and commercials. We're an overabundant group of individuals at sleep within the matrix of "I Want More!" Choices are made for us while allowing the perception that we made the decision. Everything we see provides an external source for providing it to us, and thus, no original thought.

Psychiatry is a religion where the pill is worshipped for the freedom it brings, and psychotherapists provide answers and direction, not teaching and knowledge. Philosophy, however, conjures thought and practice. It is a science within a discussion for which answers are proven and disproven through . . . *action.*

Our thoughts manifest into the subconscious as memory, which is then manifested through the body (or actions of the body). One day, you can be on a street corner begging for change and the next mastering the ability to climb a mountain, levitating adjacent to the rising sun. Manifestation depends on what you choose to tell yourself, but change comes with the understanding that *no one can be reborn without going through pain.*

But the external gods many of us so often choose to worship take that power of choice away. Yes, they take the pain away, but they also rob us of our God-given right to evolve. By taking pills or having endless transactions with a therapist whose motivation is to help but not to inspire, and to tell us what to do instead of guiding us to solve riddles and puzzles on our own, we're robbing ourselves of satisfaction and personal evolution. We're denying ourselves the satisfaction and sense of accomplishment that come once the answer is brought into awareness.

No one person is greater than the next; there are only different levels of awareness, and those who are aware have the duty (to those who seek awareness) to provide knowledge and know-how with resolve to action on the part of those seeking awareness.

Philosophy reigns supreme in that we never feel more alive than when expressing an opinion and an understanding of the argument against us. These beautiful debates bring awareness to both sides. To quote Socrates (which is actually quoting Plato, as philosophy scholars would argue that Socrates never actually said anything): "One thing only I know, and that is that I know nothing." Meaning, nothing can be proven or disproven in the discussion of meaning, God, religion, and philosophy; they are all just ideas, and we all have them. Express at will; the endless debate continues because nothing is set, the universe is forever changing, and so is our awareness of those changes, both within and outside of the body; they exist in connection with each other.

To be truly aware takes discipline and patience with an understanding that our minds seek out what we desire, but that this desire is a choice. We can choose a better desire for ourselves and for the people we connect with daily. Inject a stream of consciousness into your workplace; think peace always and wish for peace and love to enter the hearts of all who surround you. Harbor no ill will toward each other, and manifest this in your actions; tell others how you appreciate their contribution because it takes many to create a whole. Sense in your bones the vibrations filled with enlightenment and awareness, and you shall see how this thought process infects those you sit with. You'll enjoy such a strange fulfillment and become accustomed to allowing the universe to run itself, and you'll be satisfied that you controlled your thoughts and actions and influenced society in not committing a great cosmic blunder headed toward a greater outcome for those waiting in line.

—*P.D. Alleva*

3

ANCIENT GREEK PHILOSOPHER-PHYSICIANS AND EARLY FOUNDATIONS OF *SPIRITUAL GROWTH THERAPY*

Speak out, do not hide inside. If you want a healer's help, you must first uncover the wound.

—PHILOSOPHIA THE PHYSICIAN

There is a wealth of historical evidence supporting the spiritual origins of the healing arts, which include medicine. Though modern historians often credit the birth of modern medicine to Hippocrates, the fifth-century BCE physician from Cos, in many ways these achievements actually belong to the mathematician Pythagoras, the sixth-century BCE sage who emigrated from his native Samos and established a community in Southern Italy. There, he founded a center that emphasized above all the three sciences of music, medicine, and divination (Guthrie 1988), all of which were designed to heal the body and purify the soul through the harmony of numbers. Pythagoras also reputedly coined the term *philosopher*, defining it as one who was able to reveal and understand the unifying (though sometimes hidden) mathematical patterns that underlie physical forms, especially those in nature. This ushered in the Axis Age of scientific reasoning about nature (*phusis*) through empirical observation and also philosophical and spiritual verification of the soul (*psuche*) through mathematical and musical proofs. *Philosophia,* according to the Pythagorean tradition, was a purification (*catharsis*) of the body to purify the soul. Thus was the foundation of Greek medicine according to the traditions ascribed to Pythagoras.

Following in this philosophical tradition are three other early fifth-century BCE philosopher/physicians of renown: Alcmaeon and Philolaus of Croton, and Empedocles of Sicily. Tied to the Pythagoreans by tradition, each has made contributions to the fields of healing and medicine that continue to this day.

Alcmaeon was the first physician to declare the brain to be the seat of intelligence as well as the center of sensations, and that these two functions were discrete. He also defined health as equilibrium of forces within the body: *homeostasis.*

Philolaus was the first to develop a distinction among the sensory, animal, and vegetative functions in the body (Sarton 1952). He localized these functions in the brain (sensory), heart (animal), and navel (vegetative) areas.

Although Galen is credited as the forefather of the model of medicine known as the Four Humors, it was Empedocles who established a medical model based on the four "root elements" of earth, air, fire, and water as constituting the composition of the human body, as well as all of nature (Sarton 1952). *Health* was a condition of these elements established in equilibrium within the body.

Hippocrates is perhaps the most recognizable name among the early Greek physicians, for even today, physicians recite the famous *Oath* attributed to him and the school that he established at Cos. Likewise, those in the healing professions still abide by the ethical principles contained in that *Oath*, for those ideals continue to serve as the gold standard for best clinical practices: first do no harm; maintain confidentiality; treat patients with respect.

The model of Philosophy as healer waned by the early sixth-century CE, when Boethius personified her in his famous work, *The Consolation of Philosophy*, in her tattered robes amid an uneducated and barbarous mob. But despite the image, here too the method was preserved, and it leaves for us the immortal fabric with which we may regather the fragments to become whole again as an immortal species.

—*Maria Maddalena Colavito*

PART TWO

FOOD FOR THOUGHT: PHILOSOPHICAL CONCEPTS FOR HEALING

4

You Are
What You Think

I think, therefore I am!
—René Descartes

The question is, who are you, or even better, who do you project yourself to be? What do you wish to be, to feel, to embody, and to project? These are the age-old questions. In turn, the answer is quite simple: who do you wish to be? As time goes on and we have experiences that give us information on who we are not, or who we choose not to be, the question is, how does all this work?

The answer is simple: what we think is who we are; our conscious thoughts (our mind) are strengthened in our subconscious (our brain), which manifests in the body (or our action). The point of true change comes in two ways: developing new behavior patterns conducive to how we see ourselves, which in turn change subconscious patterns manifesting in a change in conscious thought. Or changing conscious thought until such time as our actions mirror these thoughts. Either way, the power of action and thought is clear and present.

This chapter, and in turn, this book, is written for anyone who is tired of the endless loop of hell created from trying to live up to societal expectations. We are not sheep, and we are not slaves bent on the worship of something greater. We are a part of everything, and everything stems from what we project the universe to be. There's nothing we can't create or destroy, nothing we can't stop or start. The trick is in deciding who we want to be; my sincere hope is that your answer is *to be an enlightened, peaceful existence.*

The only limitations in this life are the ones we impose on ourselves. Even death is a limitation; in a conscious reality, there is no death; it is merely an expectation. We travel a long road leading to an ultimate awareness. Death is merely a choice of what we expect. Do you want to live forever?

When you think about tired, brittle bones, constricted lungs, and slipping thoughts, why would you want to live forever? Surely you would not if you had to endure such pain. But what if your expectation of growing old was to feel glorious, full of vigor, and to have a youthful existence?

Too often we spend our days trying to beat the clock, racing toward the finality of death with the hope that there will be no pain, and even that is an expectation. Popular culture serves up the idea of "no pain, no gain," but our awakening lies within, waiting to be shaken and aroused. As spiritual beings longing to grow more fully, more deeply, our spiritual lives are a series of small awakenings. As we are reborn in the spirit, a radical and frightening experience, it can feel like a kind of death, which is in itself a transformation. When we have recourse to being born, death becomes a transformation. But what will you do with the days and the nights that slip by almost endlessly without deep thought? We have the ability to create castles and lands and countries, worlds and solar systems and universes. The final pain leads to infinite awareness and is again a choice.

So how are our thoughts molded? Experience opens the lock of perceptions and beliefs. For instance, let's say that when you were a child, your father berated you on a daily basis with negative, disempowering verbal abuse. And let's go further to say that good old daddy was a drunk who suffered from bipolar disorder and cycled through periods of mania and extreme depression. To assume that you would grow up angry, depressed, full of low self-esteem, a nonbeliever, and even possibly a drunk is an understatement.

But your soul chose this life, this dad, this situation, for a karmic lesson to evolve from. Did your spirit choose to be an angry individual because life threw you a curveball? Anger is a devolved emotion, primitive in its essence. When the mind is free, the collective entities of the universe gather together to open and explore its intricacies with an admiration filled with joy and love. There can be no karmic reaction without recourse to pain.

The world is yours. Own it, but leave it in a better place than where you received it. When we command greatness, peace, and beauty, we receive it. The universe can never deny us our claim; it doesn't know how. It sends us exactly what we believe, so don't allow your thoughts to betray you. Purity of spirit is delivered once all our worldly attachments are stripped from our thoughts. But you must believe because without belief, nothing can ever be surpassed, changed, or accomplished. Take the athlete who is hell-bent on winning, angry that others are cheating to win and wanting nothing more than to show everyone how to win with grace. Mohammad Ali, Michael Jordan, Derek Jeter are all athletes who project greatness. How? They believed, and their actions solidified that belief. The desire to win and win big time and time again, even after defeat writhes in our hearts, is the mark of a true champion.

So what of the disempowered, the angry and the meek? Shall they inherit the earth? What a disempowered world that would be. Let's begin to awaken. There's no way past the simple truth that you either choose to change or you choose not to: there's no in-between. To those who choose to change: congratulations. The universe just breathed a celestial sigh of relief because it needs your help so it may project itself into peaceful cosmic rationale. From here, let's begin to become aware and change what we think of ourselves.

POWER OF THOUGHT

Our thoughts are powerful, perhaps the most powerful influence in the universe. We change thoughts by initiating new actions that allow us to develop new behavior patterns that then change our perception. If your thoughts betray you, and life is not satisfying, you need to change your thoughts—that's where real change comes from. Negative or positive, it's up to you. You have the power to control and balance your emotions; you have the power to break free of earthly attachments. The power to heal yourself is yours, a gift from God and the universe.

At one point in time, we were all an accumulation of cells in our mother's womb. At a moment during this process, God touched those cells with the light of life, igniting a heartbeat with peace and love. And when this process occurred, all the power in the universe was given to you as a gift. Unfortunately, society deems us unworthy of this power and seeks to cloud our judgments and beliefs of the self. Why choose to continue riding under the power of society's fear? Every human being's awakening lies dormant within the heart; all we have to do is choose to be enlightened, and we will have it.

So what does this mean exactly? The battle between the spirit and the brain is won through the heart, meaning when we live with the force of love and peace (as is our birthright to demand from the universe), our awakening and evolution take a great path toward enlightenment—for it is difficult to love when confronted with demons—and the powerful struggle of karma begins.

We must accept that there can be no rebirth without pain, but of course I'll contradict myself at this moment: this is my expectation, and it is a rule of the universe as it was created out of chaos; therefore, chaos writhes deep in the vibrations of our hearts and is dominant on the subconscious level. Chaos brings us into peace. Think of the universe, exploding into creation and continuing to expand even in this very moment. But think of its center, the center of the universe, which exists at every point in the universe. There is calm in the center like the eye of a hurricane, which is calm and rational. The same exists within every human being: there is calm and peace surrounded by a whirlwind of chaos. True vibrations swirl everywhere within and without. I love contradiction, and to quote Ralph Waldo Emerson, "Consistency is the hobgoblin of small minds." Life is too long to remain consistent with one identity, one job, one home. The American dream is a sham to begin with, constructed and filtered into the consciousness of society for one simple purpose: *to keep the powerful at bay* and constricted by the thought that we are satisfied.

To be truly consistent is a boredom of life I choose not to contain my spirit with, for the spirit is like a child, visiting everything it sees with wonder and amazement. I choose to never remain consistent, and to remain stagnant at the same time. All in moderation until such a time that moderation becomes my consistency, and then I'll change it once again to remain inconsistently consistent. The most basic truth in all of this is to never allow any circumstance, event, or behavior to dominate your life. You may choose to continue to live in a disempowered state, or you may choose to awaken. The choice is yours.

POWER OF CHANGE

Let's say you wake up every morning dreading going to work. Your mind is filled with thoughts of boredom, disgust with life, and a sensation of the self that life is meaningless. The question remains: why would you continue riding such a vibration? Is it because you become comfortable?

Human beings are the most adaptable creatures on the planet, perhaps even in the universe. We can adapt to weather and environment (look at us, we survived the Ice Age); we can adapt to hate and violence, to discomfort and pain; however, we fear change, and this fear writhes in our bones, keeping us at bay. But if we are adaptable, does this not mean that we will adapt to peace and serenity?

No meager or feeble existence should be acceptable to anyone. Everyone has the right to command from the universe their highest gratitude for breathing through enrichment and a thirst for knowledge and desire for something great—greater than the self and larger than the stratosphere. Collective consciousness, when collaborated on the right vibration, leaves us all living in paradise, that grand and promised utopia. That's right, promised!

However, back to our example of you as the locked and disempowered person who woke up in the morning, dissatisfied but fearing change and what it takes to change. Your thoughts are obvious: you feel disempowered, and your actions are consistent with this identity. So how do you dive into a drastic change? Remember, the brain works by receiving signals from two outside resources: thoughts and actions. Changing either one causes the brain, the subconscious, to incite new neurochemical signals to strengthen in the brain. Over time the change that was feared becomes commonplace.

For example, I was once employed as a social worker for a nonprofit mental health facility. About two years into my employment, upper management (who will remain unmentioned in this book due to their lack of vision and simply feeble minds) decided to make a drastic change in their systematic approach. Of course, this change brought chaos throughout the facility, especially for the employees who'd worked for the agency for a considerable amount of time. All we heard for weeks and weeks before the change was implemented was bitching and moaning from every department.

Some eventually quit their employment; talk about fear of change. But the result of the change was simple: no one died, no one had a mental breakdown, and months after the change, no one even brought up how it "used to be." We are most often fools to our own ignorance.

Change happens in one of three ways. The first is over time, which is inevitable because the universe is in constant motion and is ever changing. The second is by way of a strong emotional event, which causes a change in the way we perceive ourselves or the world around us. The third is by our own volition. We choose to change, and it happens. The first two are no way in our control. Yes, we have influence over them, and some philosophers will argue that everything is nonexistent to begin with, but that is a conversation for another time. The third provides us with control and power, allowing us to rocket across the universe or die out in a cosmic dud, depending on our choices of course.

The conclusion to this chapter is simple: if your life is dissatisfying, choose to change. Change your actions and change your thoughts, and you will change yourself and everything around you with them. Be the change that inspires, and become comfortable with your change.

—P. D. Alleva

5

EGO AND EMOTION

I am the Universe; here I am.
—P. D. ALLEVA

THE BIGGEST BATTLES OF THE HUMAN PSYCHE are between ego and emotion and the balance between the two. We've all heard people suggesting we "get humble." This is a direct connection to an inflated ego; the saying *get humble* is related to balancing our emotions to the point where actions from the heart lead to fulfillment. In the addiction field, too many relapses occur as a result of a fractured or inflated ego. We build ourselves up to be super people, immortal and untouchable, but where does this inflated ego lead? It leads to destruction of the self as a result of prolonged or instant karma. We cannot continue to live with the belief that we are better than or larger than those who surround us in our homes as well as those we come into contact with daily, including the indigent on the street corner begging for change for a beer; they are all part of our connection to the almighty. We must be unassuming, however, protective of ourselves and the interests of the greater good in everything we do. So, where does this conflict initiate?

When we break down science and psychology, we can conclude that the earth is alive; as it was born so it will die. The same conclusion can be made about the sun, that godly sphere breathing fire and life, rising and setting for us every day as an acknowledgment of the circle of life from which none are immune. And what of this breathing, living universe, and what of Mother Earth? What can we surmise by this proclamation that they are just as alive as we the people? Have we not heard of the wrath of Mother Nature? Is she not alive with emotion, angry over our neglect of her health? Should we follow this course of thought throughout the history of the universe, our conclusion can be related to emotion, finite and living emotion.

OUR INTERNAL BATTLE

The universe was created out of two emotions—love and hate—and every emotion we experience is a derivative of one or the other. The closest emotion to hate is fear, the closest to love is confidence, and these are exact opposites. Look at youth finding love for the first time: does that not provide us with confidence? Have we not listened to thousands of songs describing the ways that love changed our world for the better, breeding confidence? Have we not been told stories of fear and hate causing mass destruction? How war is the product of the fear that our ideals and beliefs are challenged? That using force or hate to control that which is not in our control to begin with is a lack of intelligent thought? Part of what makes us human is our ability to philosophize and argue. No one should ever have to die because of an opinion.

Chaos ensued out of the big bang of the universe to create order. Our lives are not unlike this chaotic order. We are our own center of the universe. If we were to stand on any planet in the cosmos, that planet would seem to be the center of the universe; so it is with us. Our actions are the external parts of the universe that is an extension of the chaotic world we see around us. Our conscious thoughts are the rationale for this chaos, and our subconscious, the calm in the center. Or at least they can be. When our center, or our subconscious, is not calm and centered, chaos runs through our lives like a freight train out of control. But when we are calm in our center, we are humble and confident, breeding this confidence into the psyche of the world around us. However, there can be no rebirthing without pain and chaos, as these entities are themselves completely connected.

Well-balanced people, calm at their center, are humble people with balanced egos. They sit long enough to allow the heart to project peace into the universe. When the heart and the spirit are calm, so is our perception of the world around us. Sure, we have influence over our surroundings, but we have control over our choices. Should we begin to experience chaos in our lives, it would behoove us to choose how we will rise above such adversity, riding with the emotion we are experiencing with an understanding that these emotions will reach a calm and peace with this experience. Should our thoughts continue to switch to a negative conclusion, we must force a change by choice. "I am coming out of this experience on top," or "I am a better person because of it." These are statements to repeat to ourselves; everything else is simply a process. Every person has a battle within, a karmic evolution to secure.

FEAR

Look around you; listen to the news; what do you see and hear? It is fear. Society has deemed the masses unworthy of confidence, for what would happen should the masses turn to themselves for an understanding of life and self-healing without the need for external resources? The system is set to keep the masses under the thumb of control and accepting less than greatness. After all, there's only a certain amount of earth to go around. Twenty percent of the U.S. population owns 89 percent of the wealth, leaving only 11 percent of the wealth for the bottom 80 percent of the population (Domhoff 2013). So how does the 20 percent keep the masses at bay? By initiating practices that keep the masses believing they are less than and accepting mediocre positions that lack the ability to drive forward and receive more. They use fear as a control device and manipulate love to their advantage to keep it as far from us as possible. What would happen if one day the entire world woke up with an understanding that they are powerful and held the key to their universe within their grasp? Chaos would certainly ensue, but out of this chaos we would create a calm of the sort that is good for the universe itself.

As the cycle of fear continues, anger becomes paramount. But anger is a useless emotion that erupts from our own misperception that we must be in control of everything around us, and we feel that way because we are not in control of ourselves; hence, fear. So, what is hate other than a continuous cycled emotion holding us down on a constant basis? It breeds and cycles fear and angry energy in our worlds where a continual loop of destruction and restriction reigns. When we stop the anger and become compassionate, when we choose to open the power of the universe that was given to us and balance our act, and when we see the world through loving eyes, our perceptions of the world—and others—begins to change.

We are living in a simulated playground traveling at light speed toward a conclusion of death (which is merely an expectation to begin with, as there is no real death other than our bodies giving out). We talk about our fears to each other, visiting therapists and taking pills, aware all the time, even at the subconscious level, that the fear is really no more than a way for those in power to control us. That shields us from the truth that in the face of confidence and love, there is no fear, and the world is our oyster to mold and do with what we wish. When we choose to wake up, we hold our universe within the palm of our hands, walking the earth without fear. Society puts restrictions on us to keep us down, and these restrictions are nothing more than an imposed will for continued power by the 20 percent who hold the wealth in the U.S. But these restrictions are false perceptions. Close your eyes and dream of your life without these restrictions and understand what great things you can accomplish and what a godly figure you can be.

CONFIDENCE

Walk the world without fear, for it is our worst fears with which we manifest, and this cycle continues over the course of years. However, cut out this fear, and there is confidence, which can be achieved through love: love for oneself, love for those around you, and love for the world and universe. We can do anything when we have love in our hearts.

But there's a difference between confidence and over-confidence, or arrogance, which is a defense mechanism for poor self-esteem. Confidence is directly related to the self: you feel confident in your own skin, proud of who you are, proud of your actions today and looking forward to tomorrow where a new connection can be made, where discoveries await, and experience is beautiful and filled with wonderment. To be truly confident means feeling confident in your own abilities, understanding that a healthy mind wants no external control but to teach and learn and be wise. We must accept that we have no control other than the control of our own choices, and our power becomes endless when walking with the vibration of love in our hearts—love for the self that is dictated on how we treat our bodies and balance our emotions.

Hate is dominant when our egos are not balanced—when our emotions and our center are not calm and confident—for this imbalance breeds fear and anger and a sense of a loss of control in an endless loop that only the individual has the power to turn around. When we are able to take control of ourselves, live healthfully both spiritually (of the mind and the spirit) and physically (of the brain and the body), we are able to find the calm within ourselves and to project ourselves through morals and values that come from the heart; we are free to do anything. However, should we deem ourselves unworthy, weak, powerless, or hopeless, we continue in the endless loop. Should we begin to think of ourselves as powerful, with the healthy tools necessary to rise above all adversity, this endless loop begins to unravel.

—*P. D. Alleva*

6

EVOLUTION AND TRANSFORMATION

In this bright future you can forget your past.

—BOB MARLEY

Everything I know about evolution has come from the science books, and all I know about transformation has been received from philosophy. When we relate these concepts to the bigger picture with the knowledge of how the universe works, it becomes clear. The theory that neither matter nor energy can be created or destroyed is a powerful concept; thank you, Einstein. An equally powerful concept is that energy can only be turned into something else, or transformed, if you will. The same is true for our emotions, but we'll get to that in a page or two.

When we look at the history of the earth and observe how many times species have become extinct (not only dinosaurs have become extinct), the process of evolution becomes apparent. If we accept the idea that all energy and matter in the universe was created by the big bang and cannot be destroyed, what became of the energy and matter of these now-extinct species? Now enter the process of evolution in relation to Einstein's theory, and one interpretation is that nature, God, the universe, chooses to evolve. Like human beings do, it selects what is best for its evolution and growth, like an architect transforming a blueprint to create the perfect order of being filled with power, emotion, and at last, logic. Every dominant species that has ever walked the earth has become extinct, or transformed, just as we will ourselves reach extinction someday. So what of this evolution, or God's evolution?

The grand architect strives for balance, and in the architect's struggle to reach balance, it/she/he created humans, who are equally dependent and independent from the architect. This balance is the goal of evolution: to be in perfect harmony with all that surrounds us so the true evolutionary process can take place: greatness on a grand scheme. The architect's tool is transformation, because none of us ever truly dies. Our bodies return to the earth, and our soul's energy transforms into logic and other cosmic journeys. When we achieve the great or ultimate awareness, we are in harmony and balance within ourselves and with all that surrounds us. Now true evolution can begin to take place.

So what does all this philosophical hubbub mean exactly? All around us, every human being has his or her own personal evolution to tackle. As one evolves, the system evolves with it, and that system is God, the collective consciousness and energy of all things. Look through history at some of the most evolved souls that have walked the earth: Pythagoras, Buddha, Jesus, Mohammad; read the mythical stories that predate all these men: Horus, Zarathustra, Attis of

Phrygia—all part of God's plan and the collective human consciousness to push us to the ultimate evolution through peace and harmony and balance with each other.

For a better example of a system at work, I'd like to relate the whole system to a business. It takes a collective consciousness and teamwork to develop a successful company; from the CEO to the janitor, everyone comes with his or her own energy, and everyone feeds off the energy of the company itself. When the people in the company begin to separate their thoughts about the company's future evolution, the system begins to shut down. This is the reason a business begins to fail or turns into something different from what it had been. When there is a complete breakdown of these thoughts and purposes, the individual parts or individuals must then start over with only the knowledge of what went wrong before. However, when those involved in the company share the same vision, the same collective consciousness, the system finds balance and begins to evolve into something greater than its individual parts. The company itself may choose to take on different ideas and different directions, possibly forming new branches of the business with a collective vision that allows the entire system to evolve.

Unfortunately, we tend to become devolved due to a lack of understanding of our principle purpose and the path to our evolution. We bog ourselves down with self-defeating behavior patterns that hinder us from evolving: the devil indeed. In essence, evil, fear, anger, and hate are all rational conclusions to a universe seeking balance. But these emotions cannot bring balance alone, as there must be a single source of purpose, passion, and an insatiable desire to continue: Love!

Love is the dominant force in the entire universe, while simultaneously the most sought after force to destroy it. But love does conquer all, and for a reason. When the universe was created, it was created out of two emotions—love and hate—but with a small twist. One had to come first, even if the difference in time was a microsecond. And what came first was love. We need love to create, love to fulfill ourselves, love for ourselves, and love for all that surrounds us. We need love to evolve. This is why God always defeats Satan, why good triumphs over evil, and why the best songs and stories all have to do with love: love of family, love of another, love of each other, and love of the self.

EVOLUTION

We have now come to the Age of Aquarius, the celestial cosmic turning of the dawn of a new consciousness. This is thought evolution, spiritual evolution. We are soldiers in a spiritual war, and we must choose which side we will make a stand with. Crazy as it sounds, we are choosing a battle between our spirit and our brain, for this is a battle that is won from within, through the actions of the heart, by finding balance.

The system itself seeks evolution through balance, and it is every individual's right and responsibility to choose this balance for the greater good. We've heard of secret societies like the Illuminati and the Knights Templar having an awareness that eludes the rest of us; however, it is inevitable that the energy created by this awareness seeks its own evolution, for if we do not evolve, we reach extinction, and our energy transforms into something else that continues to seek balance in the universe. This awareness is simple: that we are all powerful, have influence over each other and the system, and come with the power of choice to be powerful beyond the cosmos. Every human awakening resides within the heart, all we have to do is choose to believe it exists, and we will find it.

TRANSFORMATION

As we are all just as powerful as the system itself, so we may also utilize the rule of transformation to our own benefit. When our lives become bogged down by an event, whether it is a traumatic event or a self-defeating behavior that is hindering our progress toward evolution, we may choose to transform the emotion tied to this event or behavior by the power of choice.

This practice happens in one of two ways, either instantly or over time, but both require continued exposure and thoughts toward the transformation process. As everything we do is tied to some type of emotion, so is the universe. We are allowed to choose which vibration we will accept into our hearts. This vibration is best explained through string theory, which allows for the process and rule of transformation to take place.

Have you ever listened to a song that pulled on your "heartstrings"? Has a movie, book, or event ever created goose bumps across the skin of your body? These are vibrations, and they constitute the universe in which we live. String theory provides us with an essential aspect of the universe that is tied to our emotions. To best explain this fact, please allow a little bit of creative license.

Picture a microscopic atom, too small for your eye to see, and yet still existing independently. Now picture this atom at the center of your heart, fluttering around on the strings of a guitar the size of the universe, where everything in creation exists on some point on these strings. The strings are in constant vibration, plucked by the hand of God or the system. These vibrations are a reflection of the goose bumps, the heartstrings, the vibrations rippling across your skin and chattering your jaw at that moment that simply takes your breath away.

Now count the strings: there are six of them, six different dimensions from which to choose, six different emotions all tied to the string next to it and carrying a piece of all the strings as they vibrate in constant flux with each other. From left to right, the strings represent our emotions: love, confidence, calm, anger, fear, hate. These are the vibrations that are dominant within the system, each of them carrying waves of secondary emotions within their flux. Of course, as a result of the consistent vibrations, love touches the vibration of hate, confidence touches fear, and calm touches anger (and every mix you can possibly think of), opening several dimensions within the system itself and transforming energy into life. In fact, they are all one and the same, and they are at our disposal at all times.

Here's a simpler definition of string theory and vibrations: When an atom is dissected, we see it is made up of electrons, protons, and neutrons. Should we dissect these elements further, we find these particles of matter are made up of one-dimensional strings that are in constant vibration. When we reduce every particle in our bodies, the air and wind around us, our thoughts (which are also a type of matter), the objects surrounding us, and the people we see, these strings exist everywhere and are constantly vibrating. Energy affects the flux of these vibrations, energy comprised of emotion. In turn, we are surrounded by energy and emotion and their vibrations. The primary flux of emotion can be fear, hate, and sadness, or happiness, confidence, and peace. These emotions surround us and occupy us, as we consist of these strings and vibrations. Which are dominant in your heart today, right now as you are reading? Which were there this morning when you awakened? Since these vibrations exist everywhere, they are at our disposal. We can choose to change our emotions with a simple decision to change the way we feel in this moment. *I Am Calm! I Am Beautiful!*

Now imagine the darkness or light in your heart. Which vibration should you choose to follow? Which should you allow into your heart? There are events in our lives that tap into these energies more than other simple moments of the everyday. For example, a person witnesses a traumatic event and accumulates the energy of anger and fear together as a response, and this energy begins to consume that person, who rides this energy into addiction or self-defeating behavior patterns that cause turmoil and strife. This person then shares the turmoil and strife with the people he or she comes in contact with, and the energy begins to take on a life of its own. Others are drawn to this energy, other people who are tapped into a similar vibration and are attracted to it because it is familiar, no matter how lowly and lonely it may seem. They become comfortable with it, rely on it, live within it. But the power of transformation is in their hands, and they can choose to filter the energy by riding the vibration into a more positive emotion.

Here we come to glimpses, which are directly related to the constant flux of vibrations within the six strings. A person who remains within the string emotion of hate will have glimpses of love surrounding him as a result of the constant flux. The same is true for the person who lives with love and calm, as she will witness glimpses of hate and fear all around her. This is why balance is so important: without balance, the system breaks down and falls into different energy, or the energy that has been dominant. We must find balance; there is no other choice to make.

But here is the trick: the power of choice can transform the negative vibration into the positive, because they are one and the same. By utilizing these glimpses of the positive, anyone riding on a negative vibration can transform his or her mood and life. Close your eyes for a moment, and think of the most beautiful moment you've ever experienced. Sense and feel the love of that moment, and when you can sense and feel it in your heart as though it is happening right now, stay there for a while. Bring it with you throughout your day, share it with the people you work with, live with, share life with, and do this over and over again until it is the vibration that carries you through everyday life, no matter what curveball the universe sends you. And when you witness a glimpse of the negative vibration, use it as a reminder of why you choose to live and thrive in a positive vibration.

—*P. D. Alleva*

7

ENERGY FIELDS BEYOND OUR COGNITIVE EXPERIENCE

We are not human beings having a spiritual experience.
We are spiritual beings having a human experience.

—PIERRE TEILHARD DE CHARDIN

The existence of hidden energies within our universe and *within our reach* can be used to heal the sick, realize our dreams, and to have a more soulful life. First we will journey through the many types of quantum and vibrational energies that are a part of our hidden universe, and then we will explore the modalities and ways we can reach out to the power of these quantum forces to heal, learn, communicate, and grow.

INTRODUCTION TO QUANTUM AND VIBRATIONAL ENERGIES

The word *quantum* takes on many forms and many meanings. At their roots, quantum energy and quantum physics are extremely technical concepts. However, it is important to note that although obscure and technically difficult to comprehend, we are all exposed to these quantum energies all the time.

Quantum energies are invisible forces that play a role in many of the things we already experience or may feel but don't fully understand. For example, consider déjà vu. Every so often, we get a vague sense of having been here before. We think the brief sensation might be from a dream, but it is puzzling nonetheless. At other times, we may feel someone looking at us and may feel a compulsion to turn toward the energy we're feeling; often, our attention is targeted on a startled and uncomfortable gazer. At other times, we think about someone or plan to call them, and then the phone rings.

These tiny incidents happen in an instant. Lacking explanation, we typically shrug our shoulders and go on with our busy lives, dismissing our brief encounter with the inexplicable. Although our quick brush with these invisible energy fields is quickly set aside, it is not entirely forgotten. We know we felt something, and we know something happened. An undeniable, instantaneous, invisible communication, not limited by mind, body, or distance, has indeed grabbed our attention and arrived in our conscious experience through some form of nontraditional energetic force. The déjà vu just flashed in our minds; the person looking at us did not touch us or communicate with us in any traditional way; the caller just happened to call when we were *thinking* about him. Quantum energy at work.

Vibrational and frequency energies are similar, but are more tangible and relatable to our human experience since they generally have a more scientific foundation and can substantiate a *measurable* physiological impact we can actually see. Supported by a large body of literature, research, and anecdotal information that confirms their efficacy, a wide array of vibrational and frequency devices can be used to manage these forms of energy to produce health-enhancing results for mind and body.

While devices that measure and support biorhythms, biofeedback, and vibroacoustic frequencies are more relatable to physiology, nonetheless they often invoke invisible quantum energies to transmit subtle messages to and from the body. For this reason, we will first explore and describe quantum energies and then we will delve into a deeper discussion on vibroacoustic and biofeedback systems. It is significant that these types of systems and devices provide stand-alone physiological and psychological benefits, but some of the devices in this class also provide a bridge, or user interface, into the quantum energy fields. For this reason, we will examine quantum energies before we describe some of our options to access these quantum fields.

SCIENCE FICTION BECOMES REALITY

How many examples do we see every day of things that used to be science fiction but have become reality? Think of flying machines, robots, Dick Tracy watches, or machines that respond to voice commands. We can explain these inventions as simply the normal course of progress due to research and science. But is it also conceivable that these fictional depictions or ideas are intentional inspirations (or precursors to the future) that are sent from the metaphysical world and targeted to select individuals with a talent (or soul experience) to offer some form of public dissemination of the concept?

Let's go further and say that perhaps these fictional entertainment concepts somehow triggered scientific imagination and inspiration. And now, concepts of pure fiction have become today's reality in the form of cell phones, voice-activated tools and devices, robotic manufacturing systems, and more. Do our ideas, thoughts, and fictional imaginations take on a unique energy signature that can be addressed and amplified and perhaps produce items that are essentially created out of nothing except the energy of the idea itself. To find the answer, let's explore the power of our thoughts.

THE POWER OF THOUGHTS

So, do we think the parade of inventions are purely random *accidents,* or are they the result of gaining a mass of *thought energy* (*awareness*) focused on a particular concept until the right set of circumstances and innovation turns fiction into reality? Or alternatively, consider various forms of *thought energy,* such as prayers and meditation that can turn sickness into health, and often produce miracles? We know that when a large number of people repeat a mantra, join in prayer, or sing or meditate together, the combined vibrational energy of the group *intention* produces an amplified vibrational force where miracles are possible.

There are numerous, documented cases of individual and group prayer, meditation, and mantras that have achieved surprising results. In these examples, the miracle of healing can be realized from the energy of thought combined with a focused *intention* to produce the desired *physical* result.

THOUGHT + INTENTION = DESIRED RESULT

We offer no proof that frivolous inventions and new products such as Dick Tracy watches illustrate a principle of natural order, but this certainly is something to consider once we learn more about the tremendous power of thought energy to manifest reality.

THOUGHT ENERGY, INTENTION, AND MANIFESTATION AS MAINSTREAM

Napoleon Hill's book *Think and Grow Rich,* published in the 1930s, is a widely accepted self-help instructional *business* book that outlines how to get rich by proactively managing thoughts and turning desires into reality. Hill discovered some universal patterns of thought (common to Andrew Carnegie and other highly successful individuals): he uncovered the pattern of unwavering drive (intention) and showed how goal-oriented thought patterns very often produce the intended results—money, houses, businesses, jobs (Hill 1937). Was his book just the first wave of commercial exposure to humanity's rediscovery of the power of the human mind to manifest reality?

Napoleon Hill "presented the idea of a 'Definite Major Purpose' as a challenge to his readers in order to make them ask themselves, 'In what do I truly believe?' According to him, 98 [percent] of people had few or no firm beliefs, and this alone put true success firmly out of their reach" (Green

1996). Hill had opportunities in his own life to put this concept to the test.

> One of Napoleon Hill's more moving stories involved his son, Blair, who was born without ears. Physicians declared that his child might be deaf and mute for life. Hill silently refused to accept the prognosis and, despite the obvious, clearly believed his son would hear some day. Not knowing when or how, but believing anything was possible, Hill's relentless desire to have his son hear and speak eventually became reality. Through persistence, belief, burning desire, and refusal to accept otherwise, Blair was able to hear and speak almost normally. In fact, neither father nor son was willing to accept defeat in this matter and also knew that Blair's affliction would ultimately become a great asset. And so it was. A hearing aid company was blessed to have Blair on their team. His remarkable story was able to bring a message of hope, inspiration, and the gift of hearing to others who might never have thought it possible. The lesson we can learn from Hill is that burning desire backed by faith has the power to transform and change lives; it has the power to manifest what we want in life. Hill himself declares that "Nature wraps up in the impulse of strong desire 'that something' which recognizes no such word as impossible, and accepts no such reality as failure" (Hill 1996).

While his book has been in the mainstream for more than seventy years, what Hill advocates is not a mechanical formula for success, but rather a formula to change the energy and vibrational frequencies of our thoughts into positive energies about the intended outcome; to visualize the end result; to know and believe that it will be achieved. His book is essentially about intention becoming reality. The entire book is dedicated to the premise that the power of the mind to manifest our desires is a power within everyone who *wants* it and is willing to direct thoughts and energies to create exactly those results.

This idea is further expanded in the book *The Secret,* which takes the formula to another level by calling it the Law of Attraction (Byrne 2006). The idea is the same: Through the power of our thoughts alone, we can manifest anything we want. There is an energy within us that makes all things possible. This thought energy, however, has the capacity to attract both positive and negative. In *The Secret,* both energies are acknowledged. Negative begets negative; positive begets positive. "I *will* find a parking spot" versus "I'll never find a spot." Here again, we find mainstream exposure to complex metaphysical energy principals for manifesting what we want.

One might wonder if the morphing of the Dick Tracy watch into a modern day beeper or cell phone was just another way that the unique vibrational energy of *thought* became reality? *Believing* something to be possible is perhaps the key to enlisting the metaphysical energies that are within each and every one of us.

El Santuario, the Sanctuary, located west of Mexico City, is another example of the strength of thoughts and beliefs. It was designed and built entirely through the guided visions of Michel Domit, a Mexican shoemaker who had no money, no architectural skills or training, and no experience in construction.

The original plans for the land where the retreat is now

located included partial demolition of the mountain to build a hotel complex. The construction of the original hotel complex was steeped in environmentally harmful negative energies and was ultimately doomed to failure. The construction had damaged the mountain, a very holy and sacred place, beyond repair (Mace 2011). Soon after, having invested and lost his money on the original hotel project, Domit was visited by the Spirit of the Mountain in his meditations and was directed to construct a spiritual retreat center, a perfectly engineered marvel of architecture in the same spot.

The shoemaker was guided on every detail of the construction through his meditations, including the exact dimensions for the structural beams and posts supporting an innovative cantilevered roof, an essential element for restoring the spirit of the damaged mountainside. Once completed, the building not only exceeded the technical skills of local architects and experts, but also resulted in a model of engineering and symbolic spiritual perfection. Every element of the hotel structure held symbolic significance for healing and was named Hospital for Souls by the visionary.

Today, the site is a spiritually revitalizing resort and university of consciousness that offers seminars in self-reflection and rebirth of consciousness while guests are exposed to nature, spirituality, and energy.

RAISING OUR CONSCIOUSNESS TO THE POWERS WITHIN

What does raising consciousness mean? In its simplest form, it means we are aware and open to new possibilities and new perspectives for living a more spiritually rewarding life. There are energies beyond the realm of our perception that are available to us, and as more of us become aware of these energetic forces within, a global rise in consciousness happens in very subtle ways and our spiritual selves begin to evolve.

Many things contribute to this rise of consciousness. We are exposed to a vast amount of information from TV, movies, radio, and the Internet. Our access to information and our awareness of human potential is more advanced than at any other time in history. People freely share their experiences on the Internet and provide information on personal as well as global levels. We are more cognizant of obscure bits of information; we share testimonials to miracles and other mysteries such as near-death experiences, extraterrestrial phenomena, the words of Nostradamus and the ancient Mayans, and much more.

The incredible and rapid proliferation of information on such a wide range of topics is educating all of us and opening our minds to a vast new body of information about things we might label as paranormal, mystical, or inexplicable. We are finding an ever-expanding plethora of documentary information on these mysteries (both modern and ancient) that cannot be explained through anything we can reference in our physical reality. Many places in the world have mysterious origins: the Great Pyramids, crop circles, Area 51 in New Mexico, the Bermuda Triangle, Stonehenge, and others. Physics and science offer incomplete answers.

One might wonder if these places are simple anomalies or if they bode the existence of alternate forms of energy or nonhuman intervention in our physical world. Portals, visitors, and other dimensions come to mind. Some speculate that there are alternate realities. Is the world we know a hologram of a vaster universe? String theory, which we discussed earlier, further explores this phenomenon.

Regardless of the theories and mysteries yet to be revealed, we can say with certainty that our thoughts are very much a part of our reality. Random, fragmented, and dispersed thought patterns may manifest a similar random path for our lives. Conversely, a deliberate, directed, intentional pattern of thought may produce a completely different pathway.

By knowing that our outward life is deeply tied to our inward life and that our inward life is deeply connected to universal energies, we become consciously aware that great empowerment is possible through our connections to these various forms of energy. Our conscious self is more aware of our own true potential—a raising of consciousness.

HEALING POWER OF SOUND

In addition to the energy of our thoughts, the sound of the spoken word and certain sound frequencies carry a signature vibration that can produce a wide array of results.

The power we attribute to sound dates back many centuries. It takes many forms, including the spoken word, meditational chants, music, drums, crystal bowls, and other vibrational frequencies. Used in this way, sound is represented by rituals that emanate from many cultures and religions. Just a few examples include Gregorian chants, ancient solfeggio frequencies, and Native American dance, song, and drumming rituals.

ENERGY FIELDS BEYOND OUR COGNITIVE EXPERIENCE

There are six ancient sound frequencies—called the solfeggio frequencies—whose energetic powers are being rediscovered. They were thought to be used in ancient Gregorian chants, such as the great hymn to St. John the Baptist (http://www.youtube.com/watch?v=1ysVC3W-G7o). The chants and their special tones were believed to impart tremendous spiritual blessings when sung in harmony during religious ceremonies. Below are the six solfeggio frequencies in hertz (Hz).

Solfeggio Frequencies

UT   396 Hz—Liberating Guilt and Fear

RE   417 Hz—Undoing Situations and Facilitating Change

MI   528 Hz—Transformation and Miracles (DNA Repair)

FA   639 Hz—Connecting/Relationships

SOL 741 Hz—Awakening Intuition

LA   852 Hz—Returning to Spiritual Order

The third frequency, 528 Hz, is the subject of much discussion and is ascribed remarkable healing powers. It is said to be the core energy emanating from the sun, that it resonates in our hearts in the form of joy, and that it is the frequency used by genetic biochemists to repair broken DNA, the genetic blueprint on which life is based. The significance of the solfeggio frequencies is yet to be understood, but research shows the energy of sound to have significance in many ways. To learn more about the sound of the six solfeggio frequencies and to hear them, search for "six solfeggio frequencies" on your favorite web browser.

SOUND AND WORD ENERGY

Sounds and the vibrational equivalent of our words can take on a physical form. Beautiful sounds or positive words, places, and things seem to restructure exposed materials into highly formed, stunning geometric shapes. Dissonant sounds, negative words, and unhealthy elements seem to melt away structure and form. This means that certain words, music, places, and things are reflected back to us by the surrounding molecules in the form of beautifully crafted crystal structures or, in the case of negative words or things, as horribly disfigured crystal structures.

Molecules Tell the Story

Using a homemade tonoscope, an experiment in cymatics (the study of visible sound and vibration) shows how vibrational tones take physical form. When exposed to a human voice singing Mozart's "Una Donna a Quindici Anni," loose granules take on various geometric shapes throughout the song and reorganize into new beautiful structures (See http://www.youtube.com/watch?v=KU84ckD1AcA to see an example, or search for Cymatics Experiment on Mozart's "Una Donna a Quindici Anni").

The power of thought, words, and music is taken to another level of "proof" in the experiments done by Masaru Emoto and described in his book, *The Hidden Messages in Water.* Included are remarkable photographs that show the impact of thoughts, music, mantras, and prayers on water crystals through exposure to Mozart's music, a beautiful sunrise, the phrases *love and gratitude, thank you,* and a prayer.

Conversely, exposure to microwaves, rock music, and words and phrases such as *Satan* and *I hate you* produced water molecules resembling discolored blobs. Emoto's photographs beautifully illustrate the healing power of love and gratitude as well as the destructive power of negativity. His experiments also indicate that words are more powerful than music and produce more dramatic crystal formations in both positive and negative formations (Emoto 2004).

Emoto's experiments amazingly demonstrate that the *energy* of words, pictures, places, music, televisions, computers, and everything else in our world is transmitted via some form of invisible energy—perhaps quantum—to the water molecules and causes them to react. Since the human body is 90 percent water, the quantum energy impact of the many positive and negative influences on our physical, mental, and emotional well-being must be considered.

Perhaps we can learn from Emoto's experiments that there are forces at work that we do not totally understand. If water reacts to good and bad words, what does this mean for the human body? Our conscious mind may not respond, but it is conceivable that our bodies are more finely tuned than we understand and are constantly receiving these transmissions. If our bodies are reacting in a way that is similar to the Emoto experiments, what are the implications of positive versus negative influences on our health and well-being?

TRANSITIONING

We might consider opening our minds to new belief systems and alternative healing modalities where understanding our connection to quantum energy fields and the invisible power of words, sound, thought, and intention may open new doors and offer rich, new experiences. These energies know neither time nor space and are seemingly able to transverse above, beyond, inside, and through physical forms. They are able to *become* physical forms—or results or events or feelings. Think back: just thinking of your friend elicited a phone call; speaking the words "I love you" changed the structure of water molecules; believing he could do it, a shoemaker manifested the money and skills to create a magnificent spiritual resort. The power is within; we simply need to begin exploring.

—*M. M. Barrett*

8

MANIFESTATION

*Your duty is to treat everybody with love
as a manifestation of the Lord.*

—SWAMI SIVANADA

The concept of manifestation is no longer an unfamiliar topic. Most of us know about the power of positive thinking, and positive thinking is the key to manifestation. *Ask and It Is Given* by Ester and Jerry Hicks, *Think and Grow Rich* by Napoleon Hill, *Prosperity* by Charles Fillmore, and scores of other books discuss the art of manifestation.

Manifestation consciousness is not new. In fact, it is as old as creation, as the Bible states, "In the beginning was the Word" (John 1:1 AV), which in fact manifested the universe. It is described in the ancient Hindu Vedas, described by the ancient alchemists, and was an essential part of Christ's teaching: "Therefore I say unto you, what things soever ye desire, when you pray, believe that ye receive them, and ye shall have them" (Mark 11:24 AV). The power of the word has been taught and practiced for centuries. It is only since the Industrial Revolution that we have forgotten the creative power of word and thought, even though every invention in our civilization started as a idea and was, in fact, simply an act of manifestation. We fail to realize the full power of manifestation that rests in each of us.

In recent times, the prosperity manifestation movement has focused on wealth creation and financial success, but the principles that apply to the creation of wealth are the same for the manifestation of both physical and mental health. In his book *Manifesting: The Secret behind the Law of Attraction*, author Alexander Janzer writes, "In scientific term, applying the manifesting formula attracts the *more desirable* probabilities to 'collapse' into the physicality of your life" (Janzer 2013). In *The Power of Your Subconscious Mind*, Joseph Murphy writes, "As a man thinks, feels, and believes, so is the condition of his or her mind, body, and circumstances. . . . Your subconscious mind is scientific principle. It works according to the law of belief" (Murphy 2007).

We have learned to accept that concepts like success manifestation in business are part of a successful businessman's toolbox. But only recently have we begun to understand that health consciousness is essential to well-being.

HOW QUANTUM PHYSICS INFORMS PSYCHOTHERAPY PRACTICE

This book's purpose is to apply the principles of manifestation to personal well-being, in particular as it relates to mental health and addiction treatment. Just as our growing knowledge regarding the brain and neuroscience has informed and changed the way we think about mental health and addiction treatment, the new information regarding quantum physics informs how we must now look at psychotherapy. We now know that ours is a related, unified universe, and that everything we think and do is related to everything we are involved with. No experience is unrelated.

In fact, the world is all a matrix. In his book *The Divine Matrix: Bridging, Time, Space, Miracles, and Belief,* Gregg Braden states there are four characteristics of the Divine Matrix that make things the way they do:

Discovery #1: There is a field of energy that connects all creation.

Discovery #2: This field plays the role of a container, a bridge, and a mirror for the beliefs within us.

Discovery #3: The field is nonlocal and holographic. Every part of it is connected to every other, and each piece mirrors the whole on a smaller scale.

Discovery #4: We communicate with the field through the language of emotion (Braden 2008).

This view of reality changes everything, and the implication for mental health and substance abuse treatment is huge. Until now we have relied on the concept that patients are unable to help themselves without intervention from other trained individuals. In many helping paradigms, the patient is the object being helped by the therapist. A diagnosis is given, and then a treatment plan is carried out with the cure defined by the therapist. The therapist in this paradigm has all the power. In this paradigm, the patient is told what is wrong with him and then helped to change his behavior and thinking through the use of therapy and medication. All too often, the patient becomes habituated to living up to his diagnoses and ends up identifying with his weaknesses instead of with his strengths and capabilities and getting better.

To some degree this has been challenged with the recent movement for the practice of strength-based and positive psychology. But even these new attempts to make psychiatric practice less mechanistic and less negative have not changed the overall view of the patient-doctor relationship.

The self-help approach has been validated by the huge success of Alcoholics Anonymous and other self-help programs in solving behavioral health problems, where no professionals are needed. The paradigm for healing in these programs is service, mentorship, accountability, and spiritual experience. And most important, the problem is healed by the person who has the problem, and the main factor in the healing is a change in that person's belief system.

EMOTION IS THE POWER SOURCE OF THE UNIVERSE

We create our world by our thoughts and expectations. Emotion gets a bad rap in this era and is often discounted as irrational and not scientific. Yet all the teachings on manifestation agree that thought plus emotion create reality. Emotion is the fuel for creation and must be harnessed and directed.

You can learn to help yourself by simply changing the belief that you do not have the power to heal yourself! The new paradigm for healing, based on quantum physics and our knowledge of the laws governing manifestation, is based on a belief in the power of changing one's belief systems and then putting one's will and emotions behind this change process with a full commitment to the understanding that what we believe with our emotions will happen. If change can happen for millions of addicts, then why can't it happen for you?

For us to move to new paradigms of healing, we must be willing to think for ourselves without validation from anything else but our personal experiences. In this model, all helpers (especially those in the psychological fields) are facilitators and teachers and coaches, and our clinics become more like schools and less like hospitals.

In the Spiritual Growth Therapy model, we teach people to spend less of their time recounting their life stories and more of it learning how to change their lives by practicing the tools for manifestation. In this context, the past does not determine the present or the future. In this context, change can be immediate and permanent. Healing has more to do with decision making than the resolution of interpsychic conflict. When I was twenty-four years old, I decided to give up any use of drugs and alcohol; I entered a self-help program and changed the way I thought about myself, and for forty-one years I have been sober. I did not have nor did I need some cathartic insight to make this change other than the recognition that I no longer wanted to be an alcoholic.

I had plenty of issues that could have kept a therapist busy for many years: my father was murdered when I was four, I was sexually abused, and my mother married a racist who found my brown skin offensive. But in the end, I was able to live a productive life because I found that I was not the sum of my experiences but instead a product of my thinking and belief systems.

Spiritual Growth Therapy is based on the fact that we live in a non-mechanistic world. As human beings, we are not just driven by libido, as Dr. Sigmund Freud said, or the will to power, as Dr. Alfred Adler said, but as in quantum physics, we are products of an interactive universe where nothing is driven or static and the free will of thought allows us to manifest what we need when we need it—including freedom from psychological issues. As Alexander Janzer writes in *Manifesting: The Secret behind the Law of Attraction,* there are only two things we need to recognize:

Rule 1: What you attract in the outer world is determined by your inner world

Rule 2: When you change your inner world, it also changes what you attract in the outer world (Janzer 2013).

As Gregg Braden writes in *The Divine Matrix* (2008, vii), "*We are* the canvas, as well as the images upon the canvas. *We are* the paints, as well as the brushes." In other words, "We are as artists expressing our deepest passions, fears, dreams, and desires through the essence of a mysterious quantum canvas." Quantum mechanics is proof that the majority of us have forgotten that we are all angels with unimaginable abilities, that our goal is to learn to be a god by joining God in a fearless world of love. Once we understand that Spiritual Growth Therapy is ancient knowledge revisited through a quantum lens, we rediscover the power to heal ourselves.

—Phil Diaz

9

PURPOSE

*We all shine on, like the moon
and the stars and the sun!*
—JOHN LENNON

Life is meaningless without purpose. Without it, we are nothing more than a collage of robotic machines, never living up to our full potential. There is purpose in all we do. Whether it is a small task or daily or overarching purpose, we drive ourselves to achieve our goals. Shooting heroin is also a purpose, although in the most negative form. It is evil that leads to a meager and feeble existence, creating disempowerment and a loss of the self. So is any negative behavior pattern that defiles the existence of the soul. Choosing to continue living in the matrix and under the thumb of a society whose purpose is to drive economic hardship and maintain a false perception of control is also a feeble existence.

Should we begin to awaken from this veil of disempowerment, we disrupt the status quo by finding purpose in all we do. But there is also collective purpose of which we are all a part that drives toward a finality of enrichment, fulfillment, and prosperity of the soul. We evolve together as a society, a world society, in doing so. But what is the societal purpose? Try the following on for size: Our purpose is to aid the world in becoming a safer place for our children, understanding that this will not happen in our lifetime, but soon after we are gone. The way we achieve our purpose is through seeking balance in ourselves. The first step in achieving balance is through awareness that something must change, beginning with us.

Think of newborns and the innocence that they bring. Think of how pure their spirits are, how fascinated and unassuming. Now think of yourself at that same time, and then about all the negative energy that has come over your lifetime. Would you wish this negativity on a newborn, or would you desire to touch the child with memories of calm? Would you wish for the child to remain naive to maintain its innocence? The answer may be a resounding *no* if your desire is to protect the child from the ills of the world, the pain, the suffering, the darkness, and the disrespect with which human beings treat each other. But the only fight necessary in a utopian society is the battle within the self to maintain balance, for which God would provide the child with the tools necessary to do so.

Our purpose is influenced by the world in which we live, and the powerful struggle continues from generation to generation; most of the time, our purpose is in conflict with the acceptance that we must change. It is now that we are becoming aware of ourselves. As our solar system strives to become aware of itself, this strife is reflected in our own understanding of purpose, as we are a reflection of the solar system itself. Change happens inevitably over time.

I wish to be a guiding light, the stellar sunrise, and the vibrant colors of the sunset. I wish to be the paintbrush that carries colors to the masterpiece that drives the emotion of love into the hearts of those who gaze upon it. I wish to be the moment when a choice is made to end the powerful struggle within and to instead ride the waves of the universe into hope. I seek to understand the *why* and the *how* that keeps me from beginning to change, transforming the darkness into the powerful light of true being. I am the universe, and so are you.

I choose to be the essence, the drive, the passion in your heart that drives your hand to seek the calm the universe is looking for. I choose to be the balance of all things because that is where true love does exist. Purpose is to accept the world as it is, aware of its intricacies, rationales, and movement toward homeostasis. I wish to be the collective energy of a billion tiny moments in time, where the people come together and unite under a single purpose to inject peace, calm, and acceptance across the universe. I wish to be the thought that contemplates itself, wanting to change those parts that have held us down for so long. I wish to be the passion and agent of change in the world, moving energy into the creation of a new life in the cosmos. Here I stand collectively with the rest who wish to be the same. I wish to be the man my wife and children see in me.

Like-minded people are everywhere, wanting nothing more than to stomp out what plagues the human spirit. There is a purpose for a collective peace; what is yours? We must begin to see people in a different light and see each other as the spiritual people we are. For example, when we look at our children, it is easy to see their light, to see their godly, peaceful existence because they represent the essence of innocence, peace, and love. Our love for them is unconditional. We want to hold them and protect them, as we are drenched in their light, the light that comes from the heart and the soul, radiating outward and into our own hearts. We must see each other in the same way. We must look past skin color and facial features; we must look through the body and see the light that emanates from the heart. It is then that we can see the love that surrounds us. And in this way, our purpose becomes apparent: to unite in a collective consciousness to bring peace into the world. We must be grateful for the gift of life, for only then can we understand that unity is our ultimate purpose.

We must always remember that we are spiritual beings having a human experience.

—P. D. Alleva

PART THREE

HEALING PRINCIPLES, TOOLS, AND PROTOCOLS

10

THE ELEVEN PRINCIPLES

Having departed from your house, turn not back;
for the furies will be your attendants.

—PYTHAGORAS

When I write, the words and meanings do not come directly from me, but rather are issued to me from the cosmos. I am merely a vessel for which universal information is passed; it has always been this way for me. One day long ago, an idea floated into my thoughts that became the Eleven Principles, and the heart of Spiritual Growth Therapy. This happened on a day when I desperately wanted to understand my own behavior and to live a life that was full and meaningful—meaningful not just to myself, but to my family and the people who trusted me with their lives. The answer was given to me in the principles, which I ignored, more than likely due to being in a state of narcissism. My thought was that I would live by this code at a later date (to be assigned by myself) so that I could continue living in the manner I thought fit. But the universe doesn't work that way, and my family and I have paid the ultimate price.

LESSONS FROM THE UNIVERSE

A confession: my ego has always been larger than the universe itself; I believed that I've always been above all cosmic rationale, able to ignore what I thought did not pertain to me as long as I continued to help others. But you can't help others or yourself without heeding warnings. I ignored all the signs, and believe me, there were tons of them floating around in every place I looked or turned toward. I am, without a doubt, the biggest piece of garbage that ever walked the earth, and the principles confirm this, for anyone not following the principles is destined to learn them by force. Understand that the universe loves to teach lessons, and if we choose not to listen, it teaches again and again until, eventually, it forces us to learn them the hard way.

I have always searched for what is truly God; is he a man with a long beard who sits on high with a long walking stick, making commands and dictating practice? This concept just never grabbed hold of me. My education was filled with science classes, and I yearned to understand and combine the teachings of science in relation to God; as a philosopher, I've come up with more than a few answers—too many to share in this book. But the one I like best is simple: God is the collective consciousness of the universe, the connection between all things. What God wants is to be happy, to evolve, appointing positions to certain people, places, and things where energy is created, and dictating the practices of those within it. With this concept in mind, I must apologize to those closest and farthest from me; I allowed negative, angry energy to flow into the universe with the understanding that I am here to bring peace into the hearts of those who surround me. So please, take a warning before continuing to read.

TAKING ACTION

The warning is simple. It is related to the instruction of Pythagoras and the quote that begins this chapter, and I knew the instruction soon after writing the principles. Once you become aware of these principles, you must live and abide by them, for if you do not, the universe will teach you these principles the hard way; believe me, the hard way is not the way you want to choose. The concept is simple: You don't know what you don't know, but when you do know, you must take action. So, if you are not ready, please skip this chapter and come back to it when you know in your heart that you are ready to take action to live by the principles, because living by them takes balls of steel. But I promise that living them will lead to beauty in everything you see. I speak from personal experience: once you've committed and chosen to follow through with these principles, enlightenment and awakening are yours.

I was once involved in a discussion about what could truly be considered greatness. Most of my peers defined greatness as an action that all the world could see and agree on. After careful thought, however, my answer was more basic: "Greatness is the ability to recognize beauty in the moment that it is created!" Meaning, once we recognize the beauty in what we are given and what we see every day—to seek it, to be aware of it, and most important, to never ignore it but to live by it—we have achieved greatness.

So it is with the Eleven Principles, for the purpose of this book is to help those reading it to become evolved human beings, and an evolved human always recognizes beauty. Beauty drives our hearts to do good by others and project this beauty through our actions so the universe and the collective consciousness can breathe a sigh of peace from the anger and hate that filters through its stream of thought. We are here to balance this act and to (hopefully) one day change the vibration and tide of the universe into a peaceful and compassionate world that is filled with love. Anger and hate are primitive, devolved emotions and need to be no more. I choose to follow these principles, to embrace the signs, and to be aware of myself, my thoughts, and my actions, so that I can be on God's side and make the world a better place, for my wife, my children, my family, and for you.

With all this said, I now present you with the Eleven Principles and an explanation for each one:

THE ELEVEN PRINCIPLES

1. Always seek and strive for balance: pray and meditate daily. Beware external materialism that disconnects the mind from the spirit.

2. Display integrity and honesty in your work and private life.

3. Treat your body as a temple: eat healthy foods and stay active.

4. Connect with nature daily: take time to notice the beauty of nature and the universe, and you will find that beauty within yourself.

5. Do *not* judge; accept and perceive the world through another's eyes and heart; do not do unto others as you would not have done onto you.

6. Above all, preserve childhood innocence: treat every child with love and affection; model morals and values in your own actions.

7. Always pursue your passion.

8. Maintain connection with the universe through creativity: read and/or write daily, and tap into an artistic influence daily to recognize the beauty of the soul.

9. Display always the confidence to walk through the doors of personal evolution: have the ability to recognize the signs of your soul's desire to overcome challenges.

10. Recognize that nothing is in your control other than the choices you are presented with in the moment. Understand that there is a lesson to be learned in every decision you make; if you choose to ignore the lessons of personal evolution, the universe will teach you this lesson by force.

11. Think peace always.

PRINCIPLE #1

Always seek and strive for balance: pray and meditate daily. Beware external materialism that disconnects the mind from the spirit.

Understanding that the universe constantly seeks to balance itself, we must do the same. We are human beings, and at our core are our emotions, with which we feel and express just about every action and decision we make. A well-balanced person is someone who has his or her emotions in check, and prayer and meditation help us to achieve this status.

The principle aspect of this balancing act is the acknowledgment that as the universe progresses, as the earth travels around the sun, and as the universe spins its celestial course, our emotions are constantly being challenged and spun off balance. We must also accept that true balance is achieved in small increments and never remains for too long, which accentuates our need for seeking this balance daily.

Meditation can take many forms. True, concentrated meditation calls for a relaxed, quiet setting; however, this is often difficult to put into practice, considering how hectic our lives can be. However, meditation can be as simple as taking ten minutes a few times a day to decompress and allow the mind to process the events of the day and to use rationale and logic to assess our actions and emotions. We can also take a few minutes in the morning to listen to music and go for a walk, and sit quietly at the end of the day to reflect. These are all forms of meditation. We spend most of our days in a constant state of action, always on to the next task. However, we must be mindful of our thoughts, our emotions, and ourselves. We are not robots, but celestial beings of light: choose to stay with the light, and your life can balance itself.

As a little tip on meditation before you begin, think of who you are and what you want to achieve within yourself, and then assign a color to this thought: blue, purple, white, and always beautiful. Tell yourself an *I Am* statement: I am a fantastic mother; I am the best at my job; I am a peaceful projection of the universe; I am an enlightened and luminous being capable of turning the world into a peaceful serenity. Once you've projected your *I Am* statement, close your eyes and place yourself within the light you have chosen. Allow it to cover your body; feel it rising within your heart, cleansing your emotion and your mind. Experience the peaceful vibration plucking the strings of your heart that is projected from the heart and fluttering every cell in your body with a peaceful serenity. Now, drift above the earth, into the cosmos, becoming larger than the galaxy, larger than the stratosphere, and command your statement from the universe. Stay there a while; you'll enjoy it. It's an incredible place to be.

The second part of this principle is simply an explanation of what not to do. Technological advancement is a beautiful aspect of our current culture; however, too often we place considerable energy on wanting or believing we need such items. When we tell ourselves we need material objects, we are telling ourselves that we lack something within. Truly and honestly, we don't need any of it. When we are constantly focused on external, material items—our phones, iPods, cars, and other possessions—we forget about who we are on the inside; we forget to balance ourselves. We forget to pray and meditate; we forget we are luminous beings, and we become concrete and robotic and easy to control. We begin to treat such things as though they are God, forgetting to worship the connection between all things and spirits. Picture the addict, hell-bent everyday on finding a fix, worshipping a pill, a drink, a line, a glass pipe. How easy is a one-track mind to control; quite the zombie, as you may already know.

The warning against worshipping material items is directly connected to the first part of the first principle: pray and meditate daily. When we follow the first part, our desire for material items wanes. The art of manifestation, which begins with a thought and feeling commanded by the universe, assures us that all we require will be given to us.

PRINCIPLE #2

Display integrity and honesty in your work and private life.

This principle is simple and straightforward. Integrity is the discipline of saying what you mean and meaning what you say. Integrity is staying true to your word. At one time, a person's word was as good as a legal contract is today, and we should lament that we can no longer rely on each other to do the right thing. Should we fail in our endeavor when trying to do the right thing and it doesn't work out, so be it. Life has its ups and downs, but we must maintain our integrity as a society. We can no longer afford to be dishonest.

PRINCIPLE #3

Treat your body as a temple: eat healthy foods and stay active.

Would you taint God's universe? Would you soil and desecrate something pure? Would you walk into a place of worship and piss all over the floor? The third principle is a compilation of the first two with a little something extra. The entire universe and all its power exist within a microscopic cell within the center of your heart. When we remain stagnant and unmoving, the cell has no evolution, no depth; and this is a horrible place for the universe to be, especially when we perceive the world through frightened eyes. Get up, stand up, treat your body with respect. We must constantly feed our minds knowledge and experience and treat our bodies like a sacred temple, guided by the delicate understanding of a healthy mind. We've all heard the old adage,

"Sound mind, sound body," and the reverse is also true. It takes action—healthy action—to respect the body.

Stay away from fast food, fillers, and hormones in your food. Stay away from poisons that create angst in the body. Everything in moderation. The message is simple: if you're smoking marijuana on a daily basis, where do you believe this will take your brain? Drinking alcohol everyday? You should take a look at your liver over time. We pay for our actions as we get older. The soul may be forever, but the body is not, and your heart holds the key to the universe. Forever changing as the universe is, we are its mirror reflection, and what we do projects into the universe to sculpt and evolve it. We have the opportunity to lead multiple lives; we have the ability to take on challenges of fascination and interest. We must never remain stagnant, and how could we, with all that life has to offer? It's a sin to not progress, a sin to not evolve, a sin to not seek different experiences and interests. You were born, and one day your body will surely give out, but what will you do with the time in between?

PRINCIPLE #4

Connect with nature daily: take time to notice the beauty of nature and the universe, and you will find that beauty within yourself.

A great time spent is one where nature is present. Have you ever watched the sunrise? Have you listened to the ocean, or looked over the snowcapped mountains as you breathed the crisp, clear winter air. What rose in your heart at that time? I hope it was peace, love, and calm. Now a question:

Do the animals we share this earth with receive the same sensations? An animal rights activist could argue that they do, but just humor me here for a minute: more than likely they do not, and why is that? Perhaps because human emotions are varied and numerous. These emotions exist inside of us, and that is why we see, feel, and express them when in nature. Take a moment to sit; allow some time to reflect. Our ancestors lived in nature, and their souls were connected to the universe in a way that we strive for today, whether we acknowledge it or not. They were more connected with the universe because they were one with nature, living in a balanced harmony with their surroundings. Nature speaks to us in ways that deliver the spirit from adversity. Utilize it, for it surrounds us everywhere.

Look at the blue sky above, or, even better, the gray, overcast clouds, and view them with the knowledge that the sun still shines behind those clouds. The wind is a teacher of calm, cleansing the spirit; and the birds chirping, they chirp for you. Again, stop moving all day and take time to decompress. If your day's been annoying with challenges every minute, *stop,* breathe, take a look around, and settle your nerves. Practice this task three or four times a day until it becomes woven into the fabric of your DNA.

PRINCIPLE #5

Do *not* judge; accept and perceive the world through another's eyes and heart; do not do unto others as you would not have done onto you.

This just might be the hardest principle to follow. We make

judgments on an everyday basis as we talk and move around. We concoct thoughts about how the world should be, about how we believe people should act and display themselves. Walk a thousand miles in another man's shoes to really find out who he is. We are not here to judge; we are not here to force people to live up to our perception of how to be. This is their journey, not ours . . . although we may share in their journey should they choose for us to do so.

Human beings rarely learn through listening; our own desires are satisfied through observing the actions of others, which we select and twist to make them work for us. We never truly manipulate anyone more than we manipulate ourselves

The best any of us can truly do is to exemplify our morals and values through action. Should you not wish to be treated a certain way, than do not treat others in that same way. If you don't want people to judge you, then cease judging others. Should others seek you out for answers, offer your best advice according to your own practices and beliefs, but do not judge them should they not incorporate your advice. Look at others through compassionate eyes.

PRINCIPLE #6

Above all, preserve childhood innocence: treat every child with love and affection; model morals and values in your own actions.

We are ourselves children. The key to the fountain of youth is to maintain a young heart. The innocent look at the world with wonderment and amazement, and everything presented is of personal magical interest. This principle is not just about treatment of children, but also to preserve our own childhood innocence. Learn the lessons of the child, and remain unassuming, affectionate, amazed, and, of course, innocent.

We adults have an obligation to protect innocence no matter what has happened or occurred in our own lives. I have developed a concept, *imprinting,* which is the accumulation of energy that affects those around us. For example, consider the parents who use marijuana, hiding it from their children as a way to protect them. Ironically, these are the same parents who can't smell their child smoking pot on the other side of the house because their own pot stink resonates in their noses. Hence, imprinting has occurred. Neither parent nor child knows what the other is doing, but it has happened despite the parents' ploy to hide their behavior from the child. This practice does not protect innocence: it desecrates it.

It is the same for the energy of anger, fear, love, and compassion, as the child is open to all forms of energy. Becoming comfortable with such actions and emotions, children become adults with these practices secured in their everyday actions. What do you wish to pass on to your child? To all the children of the world? This is not to say that we must hide our struggles, or hide anything for that matter. But we must overcome, we must evolve, for the ability to endure creates great character, and the ability to be self-aware leads to the evolution of the whole person, and that is the energy to pass to our children. We must always be mindful of what we are teaching them.

PRINCIPLE #7

Always pursue your passion.

Anything less than fully pursuing your passion creates energy of a feeble existence. Today there is no reason not to pursue that which your heart and soul seek to accomplish. This is the gift given to us by our parents and grandparents, who sacrificed to offer us a better life and so we could have choices about who we wish to be. We each have a gift, a special gift, whether that's digging ditches or counting pencils; when your work satisfies your spirit, it is never truly work.

This principle is cosigned by purpose, which was entertained in a previous chapter. For who are we without purpose? What is life without passion? When we delete these two concepts from our lives, an energy begins to set in that all is for naught, and life tends to be tasteless, meaningless, and futile. When we pursue our passion, however, purpose is born, as well as direction, focus, and riches—riches of the heart and all that you desire out of life.

We are lucky in that we live such long lives. The median age is now above seventy, and the healthy are living even much longer than that. However, where we begin is not where we end, and the journey continues. As we evolve and progress through life, our interests begin to change as we receive new awareness. These interests and this awareness mold our passions, which derive new, even renewed, purpose in our lives. This is the essence of personal evolution. Life is beautiful, and we may lead multiple lives with multiple purposes as we continue on our journeys.

Energy cannot be created or destroyed, but only transformed, and this book is about the transformation process.
We must be aware that shifting our energy is paramount to
being an evolved soul. As new challenges continue to arise,
so does new awareness and new passion for changing what
we see is wrong on earth. With this in mind, we must always
seek our passion, for passion is the juice of life that continues to evolve our souls.

PRINCIPLE #8

**Maintain connection with the universe through creativity:
read and/or write daily, and tap into an artistic influence
daily to recognize the beauty of the soul.**

God is the grand creator, an artist, architect, and scientist,
and we were created in *His* image. What does that tell you
about us? That we are all powerful, compassionate, and creative. We reproduce, build cathedrals in honor of ourselves,
and paint landscapes of beauty and love. Our ability to create artistically, to recognize and acknowledge the beauty of
another's soul, sets us apart from every dominant species
that has ever roamed the earth. It took God and/or the universe millions of years to get it right, but who's to say that
we can't do the same by being aware, understanding, appre-
ciative of the art, and patient with the process.

Reading is fundamental, and writing (whether our writing
consists of recalling memories, creating stories or poems, or
examining daily thoughts and emotions) brings us to a state
of contemplation, opening up a new awareness every time
we do so. Artistic expression, specifically in the style of

music, is one of the most moving and powerful acts of solidarity we can recognize. How many times has a song brought you out of a mood to a different enlightenment? The simple act of putting on headphones, listening to good music, even possibly going for a walk while listening, is a true art of meditation that allows our thoughts to process daily events. Books, movies, and art are simply an enticing way to move into a better state of mind, for appreciating creativity is close to appreciating the grand architect.

PRINCIPLE #9

Display always the confidence to walk through the doors of personal evolution: have the ability to recognize the signs of your soul's desire to overcome challenges.

The grand number nine. In numerology, nine means infinity, and this principle holds meaning beyond the realm of concrete thought. It is abstract and complex to recognize, yet the most simple to process of all the eleven principles.

Every human being has his or her own personal evolution. Our souls chose this life and all of the challenges that have come with it, wanting nothing more than to evolve, overcome, and dominate these challenges to remove the attachments that have held our spirits down. We can always look back on our lives and witness the moments that truly set our lives apart, and those are the moments where growth and evolution took place, moments when there was a new awareness of the self and of the world around us. The universe puts us where it wants us, providing us with choices to make and lessons to learn. Should we choose to ignore these signs, the universe puts us right back in the same place until such a time that we begin to evolve, or else it forces us to learn in the most difficult way possible. Or worse, it just takes us out.

For example, let's say a twenty-year-old who smokes pot in moderation is arrested for possession of marijuana. He goes through the courts, and the charges are dropped after completing a short stint in rehab. However, he continues to use the drug, and a few months later, he's arrested again. Ask yourself, *What is the universe telling this twenty-year-old? Obviously, to stop smoking pot, but why?* The twenty-year-old goes through all the emotions and motions about pot smoking and finds there really are no adverse effects to the drug, so he continues to smoke it. And then, a job opportunity arises, but he must submit to a drug test. He takes a filter to rid his system of the pot, but it doesn't work and he fails the drug test, never taking into account that the universe was preparing him for this moment. His passion, his soul's passion, rested in the fulfillment of the employment he was offered. And now karma begins, because he was placed on a path of awareness when all the signs were pointing this out to him in the first place. Hopefully he will learn this lesson sooner rather than later, because the soul chooses to evolve, and when a species does not evolve it becomes extinct.

Pray for signs, but understand that they usually come in simple trivial gestures. Those gestures are trivial only because we view them as trivial, until such a time that the universe has to teach the lesson the hard way by knocking us over the head and saying, "Hey, now deal with this one."

PRINCIPLE #10

Recognize that nothing is in your control other than the choices you are presented with in the moment. Understand that there is a lesson to be learned in every decision you make; if you choose to ignore the lessons of personal evolution, the universe will teach you this lesson by force.

It is true that we have influence over the events that surround us, but truly there is nothing that is within our control other than the choices we make. We teach our subconscious how to make choices on the fly through actions and conscious thought; however, it is possible that what we've been taught is wrong, and this can be ascertained by taking an inventory of ourselves and deducing how our lives are going. We should think rationally about our lives, taking emotion out of our choices and utilizing logic instead. Seriously, if your life is not going the way you want it to go, you must look at your choices and understand what it is about yourself that is not working. False perceptions of the self and the world around us, disempowering thoughts, and self-defeating behaviors require attention if we are to change them.

Our first recognition is to be aware that we are not satisfied with how things are going. No matter where we are or where our choices have brought us to, once we recognize a will to change, life begins to take on a different meaning. Now the powerful struggle begins. Enter a behavior that was ignited by a thought, even on the subconscious level. Begin by identifying this consciously as a past behavior; it does not exist in present time. Even if the behavior took place two minutes ago, it is still in the past; be aware of the negative behavior and think about how you will behave differently now and in the future. Choose a different outcome and behavior for similar situations. Practice this awareness and change process until the behavior you seek is the same as the one you exhibit—and the change will become permanent.

Our self-defeating behaviors came about through years of practice, becoming subconscious reactions or automatic responses. I try not to concern myself with automatic responses once the awareness and desire for change has been chosen; our brains are on automatic pilot and must unlearn what has been learned. The discipline of time and patience leads to everlasting change to more positive behaviors.

Changing our thoughts and behaviors is best implemented with an understanding of time, which is relative to our perception. Should we choose to always live in the past, we are destined to repeat it; living in the past does not allow us to learn from the past, and we continue to attract our thoughts as they contain energy. Awareness happens in the moment, in the present, which is the only place where change can happen. When we think of our future, we must see ourselves in a light where the change has taken place. In that way we begin to attract the change itself, feeding it energy in the present. Our future contains emotion, but our past does not have to unless we choose for it to take on emotion. We must reflect logically on the past to project our desire for change into the future to earn a peaceful emotion in the present.

We must learn our lessons of the past, and we must make choices parallel to the change we wish to see in ourselves.

PRINCIPLE #11

Think Peace Always.

Every morning upon waking, at some moment before heading out to our cars and before we reach the worksite, we must think of peace. Every day at lunch, throughout the day, when we reunite with our families and our homes, we must think of peace. Before going to bed at night, we must say a prayer for peace to be delivered into our hearts and to the human existence. The great John Lennon once said, "If everyone demanded peace instead of another television set, then there'd be peace." Collective consciousness is a powerful tool and the essence of Mr. Lennon's quote. Just thinking of peace will allow this energy to become dominant in our lives and in the world in which we live. Our thoughts fill our hearts with emotion. Think of what peace feels like, looks like, and brings to the table. Allow this emotion and thought to always be in your heart, and you shall have it.

What are the ways in which world peace can be achieved? When we look at behavior patterns, the way the universe was created, the behaviors of Mother Earth over history, and our own teaching of societal behavior patterns, we see a few ways this can happen. But we are fighting against mass extinction because it is inevitable, at least when we look at the history of the universe and the earth. The most destructive forces can be avoided if we choose to work and change collectively for our survival.

As a side note, there are no living creatures on this planet that are closer to the grand architect than us. Of course, every living creature, nature, and the earth itself encompass similarities of the grand creator, yet no other creature in history has held the power to change within their grasp. It is our right, our choice, our command, and our responsibility to promote this change.

When the universe was created, it was made so out of chaos and destruction, but soon order and calm came from its center, its core, where love emanated across the universe. This simple fact can show what the future holds for mankind: order out of chaos. We've spent millenniums at war, torturing our souls for a piece of power that truly does not even exist. We've created bombs and weapons of mass destruction, killing machines that are the most deadly forces the universe has ever seen. We've marched across the earth for the purpose of destroying our fellow human beings, hiding our weapons beneath our coats as we wait for our time to attack so we can force our control and way of life on each other. In other words, we've created chaos all around us. And the earth has grown weary of our parasitic nature.

The earth itself longs for balance and may choose at will to force this lesson on us. The universe (the father of Mother Earth) looks to care for and protect its child, possibly hurtling chaos across the cosmos to bring the planetary chaos into order. Or should our mother grow angry and tired of being defiled by our sense of entitlement and lack of appreciation, she may conjure a chaotic destructive force of nature to destroy, without prejudice, earth's children, leaving order and homeostasis in the wake of this mass destruction.

In the midst of this chaos, we've taught Mother Earth a strong lesson: we only come together in a collective call for peace on earth in the wake of disaster, like hurricanes, tornadoes, tsunamis, earthquakes, genocide, and the annihilation of earth's resources. But we have come together in an attempt to help each other move through the chaos, and we've done so for centuries, teaching the earth that we only truly care for each other and are compassionate for each other after these disasters take place.

But these inevitabilities do not have to be so inevitable, if I may contradict myself. Again, the humans hold power in the palms of their hands. The power of choice, and the power of collective consciousness. We've been given a gift; we've been saved from Mother Earth's wrath by God. We survived the Ice Age, and we've survived destruction for millenniums, but who are we to defile such a gift as we've done so for so long? We've been given chance upon chance, opportunity after opportunity. We've been shown sign after sign and have ignored all calls for action with the exception of the very few. How ironic that after the appearance of our collective compassion in the wake of destruction, we return to our same hate within weeks. We return to our same disregard for each other. These actions have accumulated energy of mass destruction, energy that has grown a life of its own and wishes to breathe and continue living, feeding on fear and hate and death of the human race. But this energy, like all energy, holds the possibility of being transformed.

Think Peace Always! Collectively we can transform this energy into a peaceful existence, securing balance with the planet and ourselves. We can leave calm at our center, calm driven by a mutual existence that affords a utopian society possessing an understanding of the nature of a mass balance in the avoidance of mass destruction. Should we all begin to find balance—in ourselves, with those we live and work with, with society itself, and with the earth and universe— we'll be able to transform what we've created into a peaceful unity of existence.

—P. D. Alleva

11

HEALING ARTS OF ENERGY AND VIBRATION

*A magical, intangible process,
healing is an art, not a science.*

—ROSEMARY GLADSTAR

If the energy of a thought or idea, or words, pictures, or places has the power to manifest some form of physical response or reality, then why not consider the use of those same energies to heal the body and mind?

Over the past twenty years, we've seen a widespread and ever-growing proliferation of holistic healers, meditation centers, yoga studios, and energy medicine practitioners who use an ever-increasing array of healing modalities. The proliferation is due to a general awakening to the innate power of the mind, body, and spirit to heal the self while at the same time recognizing the severe oversaturation of pharmaceuticals as problem solvers. There is a place for each, and thus arises a new medical discipline of "integrated medicine," traditional practitioners adding energy-based treatments and other means that may work as effectively or better than traditional pharmaceuticals.

Most of these alternative modalities are familiar to most people and are fairly mainstream: yoga, exercise, nutrition counseling, chiropractic treatment, applied kinesiology, and therapies such as water therapy, saunas, infrared heat, hyperbaric chambers, laser lights, oxygen, nitrous oxide, vitamins and supplements, and many more. Most of these healing methods have some basis in physics or anatomy.

Other therapies such as chakra alignment, sound and vibration therapy, binaural beats introduced to the brain, vibroacoustic therapies introduced to the body, reiki, prayer, meditation, chanting, hypnotherapy, drum circles, crystal bowls, solfeggio frequencies, frequency machines, and neuro-linguistic programming (NLP) tap into precise and abstract energy spectrums to stimulate some form of repair. These healing modalities introduce a higher level of integration of mind, body, and spirit and include body rebalancing, soul healing, and emotional repair through energy work.

SOUND THERAPIES

We discussed the impact of sound therapy earlier in Chapter 7. Drum circles, crystal bowls, and solfeggio frequencies all provide healing and balancing through sound, which we will explore a little further here.

Most of us are familiar with more mainstream forms of sound therapy such as meditation and relaxation music that helps to soothe us into a more tranquil state. Sound machines that simulate waves, thunder, ocean, or white noise are readily available, as are wind chimes and desktop waterfalls. More uncommon forms of sound healing are achieved through drumming circles, tuning forks, Tibetan singing bowls, or crystal bowls. All are used in a variety of ways to stimulate mind, body, and spirit. And we know that music has been a mainstay of conventional spirituality, regardless of geography or culture. It has been highly integrated into religions and belief systems throughout the world over many centuries.

First, let's explore the healing benefits of music. Einstein and others tells us that the body is energy vibrating at a very dense frequency. When exposed to the vibrational sounds of certain musical notes—for example, the original solfeggio frequencies—there is widespread belief that these frequencies contain a form of energy and offer forms of individual healing and self-empowerment. It is believed that these powerful solfeggio notes were engrained in the religious music of the Catholic Church. Over the centuries, political and religious leaders somehow "lost" the hymns and Gregorian chants that represented these frequencies, and thus removed their beneficial effects from mainstream practice. In rediscovering their power, we once again see a revival of sorts in the use of the solfeggio sound frequencies for healing.

According to Dr. Leonard Horowitz and Dr. Joseph Barber (1999) these original frequencies can be used for turning grief to joy, helping someone connect with his or her Source to bring forth miracles, DNA repair, connecting with spiritual family, solving problems, becoming more intuitive, and, finally, returning to spiritual order. The belief is that these tones can assist all the energetic channels in staying open and keep the life force (the chi) literally flowing thru the chakra system quite freely. We are awakening once again to the healing potential these frequencies may represent and can easily find products that allow us to use the original solfeggio tones for our own healing and well-being.

Another form of sound healing is the drumming circle, the rhythms of which have been used by shamans and healers for hundreds of years to support physical, mental, and spiritual health. Practitioners believe that these ancient rhythms promote healing through self-expression as they produce a feeling of well-being and thus help to release emotional trauma. Drumming circles are a unique healing experience because they require individual and team participation and cooperation. Every participant is given a drum or instrument. As the drums begin to beat and the circle's rhythms come together, the participants experience their own unique contribution and gradually become aware of the unspoken trust and interdependence developing among the fellow drummers. It is exhilarating for many who try this form of sound therapy because everyone plays a part in the composition.

Tibetan singing bowls, crystal bowls, and tuning forks provide another dimension to the healing merits of sound therapy by combining sound with vibration to stimulate healing. When played, Tibetan singing bowls vibrate and produce a deep, rich tone. Many proponents claim that these vibrations can produce beneficial changes within the body by reducing stress, "harmonizing" the cells, and "balancing the body's energy system" (Wong 2013). Some also claim that Tibetan singing bowls can stimulate the immune system and produce beneficial changes in brain waves. While there is no study that conclusively offers proof of these benefits, we can see a definitive growth in the use of these vibrational therapies by acupuncturists, spas, alternative practitioners, and relaxation centers throughout the world. What's new about this is that these are ancient practices now experiencing a mainstream revival of sorts.

VIBROACOUSTIC THERAPY

Vibroacoustic therapy is an advanced, noninvasive therapy that has been used for many years to reduce tremors in Parkinson's patients and to provide clarity, calm, and focus to autistic patients and those with attention-deficit disorder (ADD) and attention-deficit/hyperactivity disorder (ADHD). It is used quite effectively with patients in drug and alcohol recovery to relieve anxiety, depression, and emotional angst. Unlike some of the modalities that tune into the energy spectrum, vibroacoustic therapy provides a physical experience of audible tones in combination with full-body vibration to accomplish induced relaxation. The delivery includes sensory deprivation—a calm space, eyes covered, and specific sound frequencies known as binaural beats delivered while lying in a relaxed, zero-gravity position. The sound is delivered through headphones and to the entire body through a special mattress fitted with high-power, low-frequency transducers. The sound provides a vibrational, relaxing massage to every cell and every organ in the body while delivering sound to the brain that induces a relaxation response in the body. The calming and healing effect is remarkable. Dr. Drew Pierson, psychologist and electrical engineer, says, "We know that the body holds emotional events in cellular memory. The use of vibration from 4.5–

1800 Hz has the effect of disengaging those resonant patterns that seem to run in loops and fixate themselves in the body. Vibroacoustics change the bioelectrical signature of the emotional imprint" (Pierson 2001, 2010). This allows mind-consciousness to have different experiences.

Vibroacoustic therapy is an extension of music therapy. A practitioner versed in vibroacoustic therapy can guide the patient through a rebalancing process using combined vibrational and audio therapies. Audio embedded with bin-aural beats alters the electrochemical environment of the brain and is used for relaxation, meditation, stress reduction, pain management, improved sleep quality, decrease in sleep requirements, super learning, enhanced creativity and intuition, remote viewing, telepathy, out-of-body experience, and lucid dreaming.

BIOFEEDBACK AND RESONANT FREQUENCIES

Another advanced healing modality that uses advanced energetic frequencies and biofeedback to identify out-of-balance conditions in the body and mind is the Scientific Consciousness Interface Operations System (SCIO) and the next-generation device called the INDIGO system. Using advanced concepts of bioresonance and direct biofeedback, the system is able to detect anomalies, out-of-balance situations, and other conditions that exist in the body while infusing repair biofeedback frequencies to help the body achieve balance and health.

The quantum nature of the energy transfer produces some remarkable results. Every organ, bone—virtually every cell in the human body—vibrates at its own resonant frequency. Together, all the frequencies in the body make up a composite imprint. The system interrogates the frequencies of virtually all of the resonant frequencies that make up the body, including the frequency of aberrant thoughts and suicidal tendencies, and provides feedback to the practitioner on the areas needing energy biofeedback to rebalance. The system then sends healing frequencies to the body in an attempt to restore the body elements to balance, or back to their natural resonant frequency. Thousands of factors are assessed, and biofeedback frequencies are passed to the body in an attempt to restore balance and well-being. The biofeedback used for rebalancing include the frequency signature for vitamins, minerals, essential oils, and much more.

In addition to the SCIO and INDIGO systems, practitioners may also use a Rife machine, another system of frequency-based biofeedback, to directly access healing frequencies for the body. For example, if someone has been exposed to intestinal parasites, the Rife machine can expose that person to the resonant frequencies claimed to kill them.

These systems have a history of controversy because the devices themselves do not have any official capacity to heal. Practitioners generally ascribe to a spirituality-based lifestyle for themselves and thus employ the power of thought in the form of meditation, metaphysics, intuition, and intention into the healing process. When used in a spirituality-based practice, these systems produce some fairly remarkable results.

INTANGIBLE REALM OF POSSIBILITY AND POTENTIAL

The limits of health extend far beyond the body, mind, and what we perceive as our physical reality. The many mysteries of the universe and the power of the mind, thoughts, and intention to manifest physical results are limitless. We seem to be entering an age of enlightenment, enhanced consciousness, and empowerment using the energetic forces known to the ancients, which are emerging once again in a reawakening of sorts. While mainstream healing continues to operate in the tangible realm, many are reaching out to the intangible realm of possibility and potential. We see thousands of examples of our voices, thoughts, and prayers affecting energy at the quantum or vibrational level, and we see that they have the power to create amazing transformative results. This is raising our global consciousness and offering an advanced context of humanity as the embodiment of our spiritual selves—and the body as the "now" vessel for all that was, is, and will be.

—M. M. Barrett

12

LEADING A SPIRITUAL EXISTENCE

Deliver me from reasons why you'd rather cry,
I'd rather fly.

—JIM MORRISON

A FULFILLING AND SPIRITUAL LIFE does not begin and end in the office of a priest, rabbi, guru, or therapist. A complete spiritual program must have daily follow-through. You will find these daily techniques are simple and easy to complete.

The first step toward a spiritual existence is to become aware that you want to or need to change. You become aware that something in your life requires your attention because it is dissatisfying and defiling. This can be a change in behavior, a change in how you think, or a change of the heart.

Energy accumulates through action, thoughts, and events. Energy holds either a negative or positive charge, and these charges are attracted to each other, as opposites are. You can use this attraction to transform the negative into a positive, but be aware that you can also transform a positive into a negative. Fortunately, you have the power of choice to help you through this transformation.

It is your perception that drives the energy and feeds the beast, allowing it to take on a life of its own. So don't feed the beast, don't allow this energy to cloud your judgment. Transform the negative into a positive with a simple thought and determination.

THE TRANSFORMATION PROCESS

The transformation process begins with a thought and a feeling, and a command thrown out into the universe that everything is going to be all right. Hope is the best of all things human. If you perceive that something is negative, you feed it negativity, and it evolves in the same way, negatively growing into a turmoil that soon explodes all over your life. But should you choose to use glimpses of positive perception to feed the negative love and caring, the negative will turn to positive and then positive will carry itself across the universe, surround everywhere you go, and protect you at all costs in spite of events that bring negative connotations with them.

The way to achieve transformation begins with the following steps:

1. Identify the negative energy: What is it you wish to change? Is it a behavior, a feeling, an emotion? Has something happened that is difficult to let go? What is it in your life that is creating an unbalance in your core, in your spirit, leaving an awful taste in your mouth that you just can't seem to get past in your everyday thinking? Iden-

tify the exact situation, event, and emotion you are struggling with.

2. Choose how you wish to transform this energy: What is the outcome you desire from this experience? What do you wish to learn? What emotion will bring you back to balance? Identify your choice for your transformation.

3. Choose an *I Am* statement: I Am Calm! I Am Peaceful! I Am Strong! I Am Filled with Love and Compassion! I Am Resilient! Your *I Am* statement should directly relate to your choice of transformation.

4. Think about and feel the emotion tied to the negative energy while repeating your *I Am* statement seven times, either out loud or in your mind. Feel the emotion of your *I Am* statement in your gut while sensing how this statement is projected into the universe. See and feel how it is projected, lifting from your gut into the sky and beyond.

5. Repeat daily until the situation and emotion are transformed.

The above steps are the beginning of transformation, which takes place over time or instantly, depending on your true desire for change. But you must believe in your own capabilities to heal the self. That you are all powerful in your own skin and hold the power of change within yourself. Sometimes our thoughts and experiences from the past create an identity that is difficult to break, as the past slips into our present thoughts like a thief in the night, causing a block in moving forward. In order to continue with the transformation process, the art of reframing and self-hypnosis helps to drive this change.

REFRAMING

Life has its inevitable ups and downs, and how we choose to interpret events means everything. Our perception of an event is contingent on how we frame our meaning of the event. Should our interpretation carry negative energy, the event will continue to consume our thoughts and our hearts with negativity. But the past is simply a memory with a lesson to be learned, a lesson that carries a logical point of view related to the meaning behind the event. Once we logically interpret the meaning of the event, there is no other reason to lend negativity to it.

Sure, there may be a call for action tied to the event, something we must do or take care of, but who needs the negativity surrounding the event? It is in the past and cannot be changed. All we can do is cope with it and transform its energy. Everyone is familiar with the old adage, "When life hands you lemons, make lemonade," which refers to transforming a negative into a positive. Our thoughts, should they continue to breed negativity into the situation, ride the lightning of chaos and disarray into anger and fear. But this is a choice, because we can choose to make lemonade instead.

The first step is to begin referring to events in the past: *I was arrested; I had anxiety; I had depression; I was traumatized.* Referring to events with a connotation of the past helps the mind to disconnect them so the events don't continue to happen in the mind; this cuts off negativity. After all, the event is no longer taking place. The lesson is what matters and what should be on your mind in the present, even if the lesson is a karmic lesson. These lessons shape your character, end self-defeating behaviors, and curb your desires. They are the events that bring a sharpness to your thoughts, a keen eye to your heart, and place into perspective what truly matters in life: the people and hearts that mean the most to you. They are the events that provide you with a decision about who you wish to be and what you wish to project into the world. Everyone loves a comeback story.

The second part of reframing has to do with the future. This part begins with a thought for the future as you close your eyes to see yourself in a different light: literally light. As you search for meaning, your thoughts move toward the future and project what you choose personally, behaviorally, and emotionally as the outcome of the event. Should your thoughts continually arrive at a negative outcome, then your thoughts are betraying you; we are often our own worst enemies. You must then change your thought of the future.

SELF-HYPNOSIS

Close your eyes and see yourself in a moment a year from now, eating lunch with a new friend, at home with your spouse or kids, at work completing a project for the day—the choice is yours. In this concocted and projected future, think about how you wish for the event to have passed; think of yourself as overcoming the event and coming out ahead of the game. See yourself in a different light. Choose a transformed you. If the event brought fear into your mind, see yourself as confident; if it brought anger, see yourself as calm and peaceful. Don't allow your eyes to open; continue to see yourself with the negative lifted and nonexistent, and transformed into positive emotion and positive thought. Feel that emotion radiating and fluttering, coursing across your body, plucking your heart-strings and fluttering your heart with peace and calm and love. Out of the heart comes the light, the beautiful, pure essence of peace. The light engulfs your body, protecting you, turning your lips into a brilliant, radiant smile. See yourself sitting there, peaceful and calm, drenched in light. See your eyes, open and mesmerized, staring in wonder and amazement and joy and love, looking upon the world with adoration and hope. Now focus on the light; feel how pure it is, how lovely and how beautiful. What color is it? Stay in this moment for as long as you are able. Allow the moment to take you to a place where peace exists. You have made it, transformed the past into the present, and it is beautiful, just like you. When you open your eyes, realize that this transformation is happening now, in the present, as you sit here, and remember the color of your light. Keep it in your mind's eye, in the back of your mind and in the foundation of your existence, for it is there always. Now meditate each morning, even if for only ten minutes, always beginning with the light in your mind's eye. Breathe in deeply through the nose and out through the mouth four times, thinking of the light and then allow your breathing to return to calm. As you do so, place yourself in a deep meditation where possibilities are endless, changing the way you think about yourself and the world around you. Try this for at least ninety days, and notice how your thoughts have changed. Then please continue for a lifetime.

Time is relative, relative to where your thoughts exist. You can choose to remain in the past, choose to exist in the future, or choose to exist in the present where the world is in the palm of your hands and you can do anything, go anywhere, feel what you wish to feel, and radiate your light across the universe. This realization is the third part of the reframing process. It is also a meditation, a self-hypnosis exercise, a manifestation, and a reality, should you choose to accept it. You are the universe; you are its center where calm has been realized out of the chaos of emotion, and where the possibilities are endless.

COMING OUT OF THE MATRIX

How do the powers that be maintain their control of power over the masses? They continually inject fear into the human psyche, feeding us the notion that we are in need of something, whether that something is a cell phone, a computer, a car, a house, a pill, a drink, or a God. These things exist to keep us locked inside a box of fear, never realizing our full potential, never understanding that we are spiritual beings with the power of the sun in our hearts who control our universe and mold our histories and stories. These things exist to distract us in the moment, where the demon is able to slip in unnoticed and control our actions, thereby discrediting us and keeping us at bay.

But our awakening lies within, dormant, until such a time that the realization comes to fruition. Awakening is as if you are slowly going to sleep and waking up in brilliance. Simply put, leading a spiritual existence is a choice, plain and simple. You have to push each day to be the best person you possibly can. And don't allow yourself to be controlled by fear.

Experiencing an awakening is like being reborn: it's painful, and it involves some sort of chaos. It is cold and uncomfortable, unfamiliar, lonely, and scary. But above all

things, it is beautiful, and brings forth amazement and wonder and—at last—freedom. The rebirth carries with it a light
that holds the heart together. The energy of the past appears
to stick every knife in your back, but those are not knives
looking to kill off your spirit; they are angels touching your
soul with a kind hand, lifting you above all that had attached
to you and freeing you of your attachments to the past to
clear away those instances that kept you within the matrix,
heavy hearted and filled with fear. The only difference in
this rebirth is that you continue on with all the knowledge
from the past so you can clear your mind to make the best
decisions you possibly can in the present.

We must rid ourselves of the attachments that cloud the
heart so that we may be free in the present.

DECOMPRESSION

We spend our time thinking, mulling over thoughts, events,
and actions, and trying to make sense of them. Our brains
rack up possibility after possibility as they react with neuro-
chemicals bouncing in our skulls. But our thoughts are like
little children needing attention to be processed.

So many people I come into contact with complain that
they just can't get the negative thoughts out of their heads.
They involve themselves with action every minute of the day
to push those thoughts aside, and when I ask them to meditate, they tell me they can't because they can't clear their
minds. They say they can't sleep because they toss and turn
all night thinking. But they've been taught incorrectly about
meditation.

How can you clear your mind when your thoughts continuously get in the way? As a simple exercise, we must give our attention-seeking children—our thoughts—the attention they require. This is the art of *decompression,* leading to an existence where we begin to feel from our gut, not from the brain. The steps for decompression are:

1. When you awaken in the morning, choose to meditate as instructed above; choose to go about the day calm and peaceful. Say your *I Am* statement, and use it as your own personal instruction for change during the day.

2. Every three hours, give yourself ten minutes to process the actions, behaviors, thoughts, and emotions of the past three hours. Did you achieve your goal of peace and calm? Did you project your *I Am* statement in your actions, behaviors, and thoughts? If not, it's okay, but ask yourself what happened and how you could have done better, and project this into the next three hours.

3. Continue this practice throughout the day and give attention to your thoughts periodically. By giving a thought and a practice to calm yourself with the goal of peace and freedom, you filter out the negative.

4. See the light inside the people you come into contact with, and choose to continue seeing them as the spiritual beings they are.

Once you filter out these thoughts, you clear yourself to see and feel and think from the gut, the animal chakra, the spirit. Your instinct exists there, waiting for the attention it deserves to lead you to a spiritual existence. For this is where God exists in a direct connection to your heart, where the universe exists inside a tiny cell in the heart's center, unlocking all the mysteries of existence. And the process begins by clearing the mind. Again, practice this exercise for ninety days and whenever life takes a turn you hadn't expected, because you will be tested. Guaranteed, you will be tested.

JUST A FEW MORE THINGS

Once you've chosen to begin your spiritual existence, you must exorcise the negative energies that have been building for so long. The following are sample exercises that will help lead to a positive experience, but of course must be supervised by a medical professional.

A three-day fast combined with meditation, reframing, and the decompression exercise helps to exorcise the negative. Fasting expels the negative energy from your gut, rids the body of toxins, and releases the filth of the past. Please drink lots of water, the elixir of the earth, while fasting. After the three days, eat and drink only what is healthy (fruits and vegetables) for an additional thirty days to cleanse the body. Continue this process of a three-day fast followed by a cleansing for thirty days over the next three months. Decompress, self-hypnotize, reframe, and choose your transformation to see yourself in a different light, and feel and think from your gut to expel the negative emotions around you.

Take the joys of life into your heart, be caring and show that you care, tell others your appreciation, tell your children you're proud of them, thank your parents for giving you life, help a stranger when you see one in need, and be mindful of the emotions surrounding you. These are all patterns of behavior that should continue for a lifetime and can be called upon whenever needed to guide you to positive healing and to leading a spiritual existence.

And above all, command from the universe a peaceful, loving existence, as it is your birthright to do so.

—P. D. Alleva

THE CALL: SPIRITUAL
PRACTICE AS HEALING

Here we are now, entertain us.

—KURT COBAIN

BOREDOM IS THE SIGN OF THE TIMES. No, it's not the boredom of the child who, tired of the familiar objects in the house, waits for someone to allow him or her to go out and play. Neither is it the boredom of the adult trapped in known company, nor the boredom of the body when it witnesses its own exchange of life or death. No, our boredom is even more radical. Conditioned to sensation from birth, we are no longer interested in play, company, or even life. We seem to move in a fog and mist of a lack of sensation or even an interest in sensation—or the lack of it.

The *second coming* of the biological body is at hand; we feel it is at hand, and it is our own skin, for between our senses and the world, we seem to have developed a new skin made entirely of lack of sensation, a skin made up exclusively of theoretical tissue, a skin that senses its own lack of sensation.

The electronic culture that surrounds us has stopped sensitizing us, and we have become absolutely bored with living and are at an intolerable distance from life. Some have taken matters into their own hands and stopped life altogether; others have tried quick exits through the mist with the aid of drugs, while others have tried various spiritual paths, like pilgrims on a quest for the Holy Grail: New Age self-gratification; gurus from other cultures; literal repetitions of texts of one's own, clinging to the word the way the shipwrecked person hangs for dear life to a sinking boat. There seems to be a revival of the desire for the spiritual, only this time, even the desire seems to move with cautious boredom.

Human life under this metaphysical straitjacket is a continuous series of experimentations, as the absence of maps creates chaos at the root of any form of identity, personal or religious. This indifference lets out an internal shout of the soul, affirming its own power in a reverberation of madness as its own eternal movement of eternal "difference."

The desire to seek spirit has been the foundation of all cultures from the beginning of human biological time. Are we different from our ancestors? Is the spiritual seeker today different, say, from a man or a woman of the sixteenth century? Do we have as much of a chance to succeed as Ignatius de Loyola, John of the Cross, or Teresa de Avila? Today we might be more distant from spiritual consolations and desolations than our ancestors, but we share the same spiritual skin.

The solution to this impasse is not to feel more and will more, but rather to break through the accumulated theoretical fog of the centuries that blocks our senses from sensation (and more so from spiritual sensation), for Ignatius,

John, and Teresa were as bored with the world surrounding them as we are with ours. Their primary goal in turning spiritual was not to become saints, but to sensitize their own lives.

The human concern is to live life every moment. What we encounter in the process may feel more or less, or even not at all, or even a total emptiness; at times, however, we might feel an occasional fullness, and on rare instances a certainty that a god or God has touched us, because the sensation is so extraordinary. This book is primarily for those who have been travelling the spiritual path and have found themselves without much company. This book deals with the practice of living a spiritual life.

HUMAN BIOLOGICAL SYSTEMS AND THE REPAIR ROOM

Earlier than the academic disciplines of psychological therapy, even earlier than theoretical reason and the faculty of reason as we use it in the West, *human texts* were created by the disciplined manipulation of the human body. These human texts, (that is, the systematic use of the body and other human faculties as the primary texts upon which the knowledge is received), refer equally to personal texts of salvation, redemption, myth, or medical healing. The demand that texts, including sacred texts, must conform to theoretical rules of some individual (prophet, group, church) or organization (Marxism, Freudianism, or other) is insignificant to biological systems. It is only catastrophic for the biological system—yours and mine—when the theoretical systems have social control over the center of human life.

From the earlier manifestations and descriptions of spiritual practice, from the Rig Veda to St. Ignatius de Loyola, the sacred text is searched for through biological manipulations of the body and written down in the human body itself.

Our orientation regarding Spiritual Growth Therapy will be primarily to read the multiple biological systems we embody. To determine also if we are free, that is, that our worlds are not fully determined, we must cultivate memory. The fact that we, as biological systems, have memory is a sign that our worlds are not fully determined. Memory serves the future because all futures share a common past but do not all share the same future.

It is common knowledge that human biological systems have the ability to reward themselves. But it is not clearly understood outside of spiritual practice how the size of the body of experience may be increased and thus increases the reward. The reward is proportional to the size of the image holding the body/experience together. Perception is always perception through image. And this makes spiritual practice possible, and so also its rewards. As human biological systems, we—you and I—have no tolerance for ambiguity and doubt. We insist always on scientific disambiguation and certainty. Spiritual practice is the only place we may find both.

It is now common knowledge (through scientific verification) that the experience of I, what the ancients called the I-shadow, does not form part of our experience at birth (Gazzaniga 1978, 1987). Thus, the child later discovers I-self. It is this I-ness experience that is the source of most of our human—scientific, political, and individual—problems. It either raises its head as a self, a hidden mystery, or a theory of knowledge. It is always presupposed. Yet, it is not part of reflection. I-ness sits on reflection. It is earlier than memory, and it is always presumed by memory. It is not part of any particular observation; it observes the observer. The question is how does this omnipresent shadow-I come into being? Is it also a biological fact?

Neurobiology has made it clear, to the relief of those dedicated to the spiritual path, that every human event is registered by the brain twice: once in the "oceanic" state as a not-I experience, and only later as a selective shadow of previous perception (Gazzaniga 1994, Colavito 1995). This delay mechanism accounts for the appearance of not only the I-shadow, but also of all the substitution systems devised by cultures that take the place of the experience: ideologies, churches, institutions, and others.

Boredom of the self, of the shadow, is only a sign of lack of sensation. At this time in history, it is also the sign that this shadow is the only source of sensation that seems to be available to the culture at large. The manipulation of sensation through spiritual practice may start as manipulation, but the result does not belong to the I-shadow, the individual self, even when sensation goes through its biological body. It is also a clear sign of the times that the substitution systems allowed to take the place of the I-shadow, that is, the cultural and social, interfere with the well-being of the biological systems. Science and religion, for instance, may stop being what they are and doing what they do when they operate as biological systems and become instead ideological systems or systems of alienation from sensation for the biological systems. Science, for example, becomes scientism, an ideology treating all phenomena (including humans) as objects, and religion becomes technology, an imposition of the left-brain technologies on the biological acts of the right brain and the experiential practice of humans.

The present model of Spiritual Growth Therapy is revelatory not because it is an apology for science or religion, but because it shows that the authentic path of the mystics is much closer to real science than to ideology. Thus, the human faith we share in the actual origin of our own species (particularly in an age that has been brutal in the destruction of most of our beliefs) is unified. Our primary task, therefore, is to make a clear description of biological systems rather than place spiritual signs under the umbrella of one ideology or another.

THE READING OF SIGNS

Spiritual practice is not a picnic. Nor is it enough to feel good about its practice in private. True spiritual life transcends individuals and reaches the public domain. The mystic is only the instrument for this intrusion of the spiritual into the material. Spiritual practice gives out signs, and these signs affect not only the body of the individual mystic, but also the body of the surrounding world.

There is no proper meditation, no proper spiritual practice, if signs do not appear. In fact, the test of spiritual practice is that it gives out specific signs. The second test of spiritual practice is that these signs must be able to be read simultaneously by the spiritual practitioner and also by an additional person, commonly the spiritual guide. Both must find themselves reading the same text.

What chance does the contemporary practitioner have of finding an appropriate reader of signs? Social scientists start by denying objectivity, public signs, and human transcendence—in one word, the *validity* of the project itself of spiritual practice. On the other hand, the organized churches are more concerned with the external signs of power, influence, riches, control, and the party line than with the signs of revelation. And this apparently has been the inheritance of mystics of all ages. Ignatius de Loyola, John of the Cross, and Teresa de Avila (to mention a few) were victims of the Inquisition while they never stopped searching for that one person with whom they could make a public reading of their meditation signs. Teresa had five confessors at one time, Ignatius had several, and so did John of the Cross. The reader of the sign must share with the practitioner the same primary technology—the actual embodied exercises—of meditation to be able to read. Furthermore, the guide should be experienced in reading several secondary technologies (sets of signs) to be able to read the origin of each. In the absence of this knowledge, readers of signs do more harm than good: they search for ways to humiliate the practitioner, and mostly delay healing.

Spiritual practice for any contemporary person is neither politically correct nor accessible to the actual human faculties we are encouraged to use. Our culture is primarily theoretical, and our minds are forced by training to think and think, devise ideas, follow logical paths, follow some form of reason. Our penchant for theorizing, our actual habit of wrapping the world—the body, every act—in theory has weakened the will of all of us. The will is the body affections and the body movements and mutations. The preparation for the arrival of spiritual signs requires that we first sharpen the will if any manifestation is to occur. It is for this reason that the discernment of signs is so essential to the spiritual life. Signs will appear in meditation as a result of the technologies we use while meditating, but the signs may come from several sources: some from the good spirit, some from the evil one, and some our own conditioning. The important thing about discernment is to know which is which.

Signs vary from individual to individual. What does not vary is the fact that we all interpret them—hence the need for an outside reader. And here is where the difficulties increase. Our contemporary life is not lived in communities, and the life of the searcher for spiritual practice is even more isolated. Where can we find an outsider who can read the signs?

PATH OF THE SPIRITUAL

There are many people who talk and make speeches about how to choose the path of the spiritual. The truth of the matter is that the spiritual chooses us, and there is not much we can do not to follow. It has been a common practice of the mystics to look over their shoulders to see how earlier mystics fared in the path, how they read the signs, how they managed to keep their sanity while also keeping their bodies out of jail. It was also their practice to speak as the Inquisitions allowed them with the utmost orthodoxy, keeping the real truth to themselves and to those other mystics able to read between the lines. No one is going to learn from a mystic how to become one, unless one is already one and finds in the other mystics the way to read the signs of the path.

The rewards of this path, even when not searched for, are worth the trouble. Where the natural determines for us our highs and lows, sensation for a mystic is deeper, more lasting. What the mystic calls consolation is not just ordinary or even extraordinary human joy; it is joy reaching the deepest recesses of our body and soul. No mystic stays a mystic because of lack of sensation, but rather because sensation is greater. The same can be said of desolations: they are not ordinary boredom. They are either filled with positive signs or death seems to be around the corner, and yet somehow one knows death is as distant as joy. The sign of tears is one of the most exquisite gifts; tears pour out of the eyes, but the whole body is embalmed in a sweet and peaceful sensation. There are also sounds and colors more clear and filled with sensation than ordinary sounds and colors. There is clarity of mind, directness of the will, knowledge without doubts, and an increase in the sense of touch as if the whole body and soul were suddenly tactile, and the same with smell and movement. "Oceanic experiences" are common; time and space seem to stand still or are in slow motion. Complete silence around experiences of a time before time for everything therein seems to occur an instant before it happens. We seem to be witnessing the whole thing, and there is no distinction between "it" and us—our bodies—with no shadow or agent. There is also the change in body temperature from heat to increased heat to the absolute freeze of an icicle, for the body would weaken with the emotional heat of deep intensity or would not be able to experience the enormous emotional charge of the mystical signs.

But above all, there is a deep sense of humility, for in all these experiences, the self is absent as an agent, or even as the recipient of sensation. All these signs pass through the body the way blood passes through veins. Thus, the body is not the agent of the divine nod, nor the agent-beneficiary of divine gifts. These gifts, these signs, pass through the body as sun's rays through a windowpane. There is not much a mystic can do to avoid these signs or bring them about. Spiritual practice is a gift, and so is the ascent to the mountain and even to the top of the mountain, for as St. John of the Cross reminds us, "On the top of the mountain, nothing, nothing, nothing" (de Nicolas 1989). However, spiritual practice may become a lost gift if not cultivated or properly cared for.

—*Antonio T. de Nicolas*

BIBLIOGRAPHY

Braden, Gregg. 2008. *The Divine Matrix: Bridging, Time, Space, Miracles, and Belief.* Carlsbad, CA: Hay House

Byrne, Rhonda. 2006. *The Secret.* New York: Atria

Colavito, Maria M. 1995. *The Heresy of Oedipus and the Mind/Mind Split: A Study of the Biocultural Origins of Civilization.* Lewiston, NY: Edwin Mellon Press.

de Nicolas, Antonio T. 1989. *St. John of the Cross, Alchemist of the Soul.* New York: Paragon House.

Domhoff, G. William. "Who Rules America: Wealth, Income, and Power." First posted September 2005; updated February 2013. http://whorulesamerica.net/power/wealth.html. Accessed October 10, 2013.

Emoto, Masaru. 2004. *The Hidden Messages in Water.* Hillsboro, OR: Beyond Words Pub.

Frankl, Viktor E. 2006. *Man's Search for Meaning.* Boston: Beacon.

Gazzaniga, Michael S. 1978. *The Integrated Mind.* Plenum Press: New York.

———. 1987 "Cognitive and Neurologic Aspects of Hemispheric Disconnection in the Human Brain," *Discussions in Neurosciences.* FESN.

———. 1994. *Nature's Mind: The Biological Roots of Thinking, Emotions, Sexuality, Language, and Intelligence.* New York: Basic Books.

Guthrie, K. S. (Ed.). 1988. *The Pythagorean Sourcebook and Library.* Grand Rapids, MI: Phanes Press.

Green, Don M. "Napoleon Hill," in *The History of the Pound, Volume III: People of Pound,* edited by Grace B. Edwards and Brenda D. Salyers, 1996. Published by the Historical Society of the Pound.

Hill, Napoleon. 1937, 1988. *Think and Grow Rich.* Chicago, IL: Combined Registry Company, pp. viii; 11; 52–63.

Hill, Napoleon. 1996. *Think and Grow Rich.* New York, NY: Ballantine, 41–47.

Horowitz, Leonard G., and Joseph E. Barber. 1999. *Healing Codes for the Biological Apocolypse.* Sandpoint, ID: Healthy World Distributing.

Janzer, Alexander. 2013 *Manifesting: The Secret behind the Law of Attraction.* CreateSpace Independent Publishing Platform.

King, Martin Luther, Jr. 1963. "I Have a Dream" speech. March on Washington.

Laing, R. D. 1960. *The Divided Self: An Existential Study in Sanity and Madness.* London: Penguin.

Mace, Lilou. 2011. "Serving the spirit of the mountain, co-creating heaven on earth." YouTube video 1:12:55. Interview with Michel Domit, El Santuario, Mexico and posted by Lilou's Juicy Living Tour on November 19, 2011, www.youtube.com/watch?v=gG_k5-MH7fM. Posted by M. M. Barrett at www.youtube.com/watch?v=gG_k5-MH7fM&list=PL5F68AFD06B7CBB1B&index=6.

May, Rollo. 1953. *Man's Search for Himself.* New York: W. W. Norton & Company, Inc.

Murphy, Joseph. 2007. *The Power of Your Subconscious Mind.* Radfor, VA: Wilder Publications.

Pierson, D. 2001, 2010. In J. Leeds, *The Power of Sound: How to Be Healthy and Productive Using Music and Sound* (pp. 189–190). Rochester, VT: Healing Arts Press.

Robbins, Tony. "Unleash the Power Within" (lecture/seminar, Ft. Lauderdale Convention Center, Ft. Lauderdale, FL, March 24–27 2011).

Sarton, G. 1952. *A History of Science: Ancient Science through the Golden Age of Greece.* New York: John Wiley & Sons.

Stolzer, J. M. 2008. "Early Childhood Experiences and the Development of Schizophrenia: An Existential Analysis." *International Journal of Existential Psychology and Psychotherapy* 2(2), http://journal.existentialpsychology.org/index.php?journal=ExPsy&page=article&op=viewArticle&path%5b%5d=119&path%5b%5d=web. Accessed October 18, 2013.

Wong, Cathy. "Tibetan Singing Bowls for Healing." About.com, updated July 10, 2013, http://altmedicine.about.com/od/music soundtherapy/a/Tibetan-Singing-Bowls.htm.

ABOUT THE AUTHORS

Phil Diaz, MSW, LLD (H) DACACD, is a partner in Lifescape Solutions and Let Your Soul Evolve, a substance abuse and mental health treatment program that practices Spiritual Growth Therapy. Mr. Diaz is a Gestalt therapist with thirty years of experience in the healing profession. He is an internationally known trainer and coauthor of six books on addiction, trauma, and spirituality. His work with Native Americans and other indigenous people has led to his insight into spirituality and the human condition. Formerly with the White House Drug Czar's office, Diaz has experience in all aspects of drug prevention and treatment programming and public policy.

P.D. Alleva, MSW, is a clinical hypnotherapist who has had a lifetime of experience interpreting the signs of the universe. He is a philosopher, author, hypnotherapist, and a spiritual guide. His passion for spiritual growth and insight into universal truths continues to transform his life and propels him forward, gathering and sharing knowledge of ancient wisdom. He is an owner and partner of Lifescape Solutions and Let Your Soul Evolve, and the author of three novels: *Indifference, Celestial Silence,* and the upcoming *A Billion Tiny Moments in Time.* He lives in South Florida with his wife, Lisa, his son Dominick, daughter Bre'Anne, and twins Leo and Santino.

Antonio T. de Nicolas, PhD, was educated in Spain, India, and the United States. He is professor emeritus of philosophy at the State University of New York at Stony Brook. Professor de Nicolas is the author or editor of forty books. Though a philosopher by profession, Dr. de Nicolas confesses that his most abiding philosophical concern is spiritual imagining, a subject that he has articulated most recently through poetry. He is presently a director of the Biocultural Research Institute located in Florida. He has recently completed two new manuscripts: Homer, *The Odyssey* (cotranslated in verse from the Homeric Greek), and *Boethius, The Consolation of Philosophy* (translated with commentary).

Maria Maddalena Colavito, PhD, is a professor of philosophy and humanities. Her employment background includes thirty years of clinical and administrative experience in positions in the private sector, higher education, and social services, most recently as director of St. Johns County Health and Human Services in Florida. Dr. Colavito is a certified philosophical counselor and the author of four books. Her research on the biocultural paradigm has been cited by sources in the fields of child welfare, medical ethics, and culture studies.

M. M. Barrett, BA, BS, is a corporate strategist and practitioner of the SCIO and Indigo biofeedback system, which she acquired to help advance the concepts of natural energy healing using the powers within each of us. She has many years of experience working with groups and individuals on metaphysical, spirituality, natural healing, and soul progression concepts as well as alternative healing modalities and tools. Her evolution into practitioner was a natural result of her long-time commitment to advancing the power of the energies around and within us. She is a member of local and international energy and biofeedback practitioner groups.

NEW AGE CENTER FOR HEALING
Pioneers of Spiritual Growth Therapy
888-765-7477

Trauma • Addiction
Mental Health

*Clinical hypnosis with spiritual growth therapy
training and certification*

Providing Spiritual Healing
Evolve Mental Health, LLC
www.EvolveMentalHealth.com

and New Age Treatment
Lifescape Solutions, LLC
www.LifescapeSolutions.com

LET YOUR SOUL EVOLVE
Spiritual Growth for the New Millennium
Phil Diaz & P.D. Alleva
with
Antonio T. de Nicolas,
Maria Maddalena Colavito,
M.M. Barrett
www.LetYourSoulEvolve.com